# WE CAN HELP GOD HEAL US

*With Ways of Jesus Christ*

## Douglas E. Busby
**M.D., M.Sc., D.Min., Ph.D.**

Cover Picture: Jesus Christ heals a blind man. People gather to watch. Illustration published in *The Life of Christ* by Louise Seymour Houghton (American Tract Society: New York) in 1890. Copyright expired. Artwork is in Public Domain. Digitally restored stock illustration from iShares.

Third Edition, 2024

Copyright ©2020 Douglas E. Busby

All rights reserved.

ISBN: 9798303658820

*Dedicated to Christina, my wife, and soulmate,
for your support of my ministry.
May God continue to empower us
for our work in spiritual healing.*

# CONTENTS

| | |
|---|---:|
| Preface | i |
| A. INTRODUCTION | 1 |
| B. HISTORY OF SPIRITUAL HEALING | |
|     1. In Pre-biblical and Old Testament Times | 7 |
|     2. In New Testament Times | 12 |
|     3. From Biblical Times to the Present | 24 |
| C. JESUS' WAYS FOR SPIRITUAL HEALING | |
|     1. Spiritual Faith | 33 |
|     2. Compassion | 36 |
|     3. Prayer | 38 |
|     4. Touch (The Laying on of Hands) | 46 |
|     5. Repeat Spiritual Healing Sessions | 48 |
| D. PREPARATION FOR A SPIRITUAL HEALING SESSION | |
|     1. Setting | 49 |
|     2. Understanding | 50 |
|     3. Mindfulness | 52 |
|     4. Permission | 58 |
| E. A SPIRITUAL HEALING SESSION | |
|     1. Framework | 59 |
|     2. Resources | 62 |
| References | 89 |
| APPENDIX A, Jesus and Spiritual Healing | 99 |
| APPENDIX B, Jesus' Followers and Spiritual Healing | 110 |

# Preface

I am a physician and theologian who became interested in spiritual healing from watching televangelists perform it when I studied medicine in the late 1950s and biophysics in the early 1960s. This interest was greatly enhanced several decades later when I unexpectedly had several remarkable opportunities to study, practice, witness, and even personally experience spiritual healing. From these opportunities I learned that God creates a "universal vital life force energy" that can heal us. Moreover, we can use various spiritually empowered ways, as shown to us by Jesus Christ, to channel this energy to help God heal us.

Before you read further in this book, you may wish to know how the words "spiritual healing" are defined. They can mean God's use of universal vital life force energy to heal us, or our channeling this energy to help God heal us. They can also mean the process of healing by universal vital life force energy. Finally, they can mean improving or curing a health condition by God, with or without our help.

You may also wish to know more about the results of spiritual healing. Improving a health condition is most often transformational in nature, such as maintaining strength and balance in body, mind, and spirit, adjusting to physical or mental limitations being produced by the medical condition, and accepting the love of God, family, and friends when approaching death from a health condition. Curing a health condition by spiritual healing is a complete healing of the condition, although some disability from a cured condition may remain.

History has shown that all people have the inborn ability to channel universal vital life force energy, some quite exceptionally. As I describe in this book, Jesus Christ showed how we can use this ability to help God heal us.

Unfortunately, many Christians have disregarded or even doubted the fact that we can help God heal us. So, I have written this book to promote a wider awareness of our ability to help God heal us. In it, I describe Jesus' ways of helping God with spiritual healing and how these ways can be applied in a spiritual healing session. I also provide information on how to design and conduct a spiritual healing session, including its preparation and framework, and resources for it.

In this book, as well as in my talks about spiritual healing, I use some descriptive words and phrases that may not be familiar to you. "Universal vital life force energy," "healing energy of the Holy Spirit," "healing energy of God's Spirit," and "divine healing energy" are used interchangeably. "Health condition" pertains to any physical, mental, emotional, or spiritual illness, sickness, disease, injury, disorder, disability, infirmity, or other condition that adversely affects a person's health, or optimal state of well-being. "Direct spiritual healing" is performed on a person who is present to receive the healing, and "distant spiritual healing" is performed on a person who is not present to receive the healing. Distant spiritual healing can also be performed in the same way as direct spiritual healing by using a stand-in person, or "surrogate," to represent the person who is not present to receive direct spiritual healing.

The biblical quotations are in this book are from the New Revised Standard Version (NRSV) of the Holy Bible, and are italicized. Standard abbreviations are used for the books of the Bible. I use B.C.E. ("before common era") and C.E. ("common era"), respectively in place of the former terms, B.C. ("before Christ") and A.D. (anno Domini, or "in the year of our Lord").

## A. INTRODUCTION

Let me begin with the story of the spiritual healing that I experienced as a teenager at the Martyrs' Shrine in Midland, Ontario, Canada. This shrine is a beautiful Roman Catholic Church high on a hilltop near the site of "Sainte-Marie among the Hurons," a French Jesuit mission established over 350 years ago to serve the local, indigenous Huron Indians and their neighboring tribes. The shrine honors six Jesuit missionaries and two French workers who were martyred there by an invading indigenous Iroquois Indian tribe. Subsequently, it became one of many shrines worldwide to which people with various medical conditions have come to pray for spiritual healing.

On the morning that my parents, little sister, and I were returning home from our vacation in Northern Ontario via Midland, I awoke with a fever, headache, and dizziness, and whenever I raised my head off a pillow, intense nausea, and vomiting. For the trip, my parents had me lie down in the back seat of our car, and my sister sat with them in the front seat. As beautiful steeples of the Martyr's Shrine church came into view, my mother suggested that my father, little sister, and she briefly visit the shrine, while I rest in the car. A few minutes after they left me, all of the symptoms of my illness suddenly disappeared. I exited the car, climbed the long flight of the front steps to the church, and went inside it. Quite surprised by my unexpected joining them, my parents assured themselves that I felt well enough to walk with them in and around the church. Curiosity soon stopped me to look inside a roped-off area containing an altar with a painting of the martyrs above it, and piles of crutches, canes, leg braces, and several empty wheelchairs. While I stood there, my father told me that they had been left by people who had come to the shrine to pray to God to heal their various health conditions. I have since believed that this sacred place was also responsible for the sudden, unexpected healing of my illness that day.

In my late teens I vacillated between choosing theology or medicine as my future vocation. The experience of serving as an acolyte in our church inspired me to think about studying theology to be a minister, and working two summers at a local hospital generated my interest in studying medicine to be a doctor. In my last year of high school, the minister of our church told a fellow acolyte who was also interested in going into the ministry, that no one should do so without first being "called" by God. I intently listened for such a call for many weeks and, after hearing nothing of the sort, decided on medicine. Just before I entered medical school, I discussed my continuing interest in studying theology with the minister of a church where I was assisting in worship services. He assured me that ministry would always be an option for me whether or not I ever heard God's call to it. From then on I hoped that eventually I might have the opportunity to go to seminary to study theology.

As I learned neuroanatomy and neurophysiology in medical school, two spiritually related questions entered my mind. First, I wondered if the soul, or human spirit,[a] might reside in the brain. Then I heard the renowned Canadian neurosurgeon, Dr. Wilder Penfield, say in a speech given at our annual dinner of the school's William Osler Society, that he had not found any physical evidence of our having soul. After giving considerable thought to Dr. Penfield's statement, I concluded that the soul must then be some form of intelligent energy in our body. Later in medical school, I began to wonder whether the soul can interact with our body and mind to affect our health, when the Canadian endocrinologist and "father of stress," Dr. Hans Selye, discovered that various physical, mental, emotional, and even

---

[a] In this book I will mainly use the more conventional term, "spirit," for "soul."

spiritual stresses can aggravate and even cause health conditions. Thirty-five years later, I found plausible answers to these questions when I began to study spiritual healing and its related medical science, energy medicine. I learned that about 3,500 years ago, the ancient Indo-European people wrote in the ancient Sanscrit language about a highly complex energy field, now called the "subtle energy body," which occupies and surrounds each human being and is sustained by an energy, now called "universal vital life force energy." They believed, and modern science has confirmed, that the subtle energy body supports our physical, mental, emotional, and spiritual health and that universal vital life force energy has the power to heal.

My early interest in spiritual healing focused on the healing ministries of two televangelists, Kathryn Kuhlman and Oral Roberts. Both Kuhlman and Roberts were charismatic personalities who used remarkably different yet seemingly effective ways to channel universal vital life force energy for healing.

Kuhlman was a dramatic preacher who began her healing services with a stream of clearly and slowly articulated theological reassurances and inspirational songs, as she walked about a large stage, raising her hands up high as she repeatedly invited the presence of the Holy Spirit. While still on stage she used prayer and usually touch for the spiritual healing of each person who came before her. Interestingly, many whom she touched immediately became weak and some also lost consciousness for a few seconds to several minutes - a phenomenon that she attributed to the divine healing energy which she was channeling. Meanwhile, spontaneous spiritual healing was also occurring in Kuhlman's audience, with her seeming to know who and what had been healed.

Roberts was a forceful speaker who began his healing services with a gospel-based sermon focusing on the spiritual healing that Jesus Christ performed while walking forward and backward on a small stage holding a microphone mounted on its floor stand. After an altar call, he sat on a chair at the forward edge of the stage, placed his right hand on the head, and prayed for the healing of each person who came before him, frequently saying that he was feeling the power of God passing through the hand.

During Kuhlman's and Roberts' spiritual healing events, numerous people appeared to have been healed, most often of impairing physical health conditions such as paralysis and orthopedic deformities, deafness, and blindness. As I marveled at what I was observing on the television screen, I often wondered whether the power of suggestion or the power of the Holy Spirit - or both - were responsible for these apparent spiritual healings. Although I assumed that the power of suggestion was operating to some degree in some people, I also presumed that I was actually witnessing spiritual healing by the Holy Spirit in response to Kuhlman, Roberts, and their audiences asking God for it in a spiritually energized way.

In the 35 years that I practiced medicine, I saw many patients who needed spiritual care along with their health care. Many times, I heard them say that their health condition was God's punishment for what they had done wrong. I often wondered whether guilt, anger, or despair caused by their believing this could interfere with healing. I often wanted to assure them that God does not punish us with a health condition, but instead helps us heal. However, physicians of my era in medicine did not get involved with spiritually related matters.

In 1994, I began to study theology at the Chicago Theological Seminary. Also about that time, the growing number of books and articles being written on prayer for healing rekindled my interest in spiritual healing. In seminary, I took a course entitled "Healing in the New Testament." To my surprise, the professor interpreted the spiritual healing events in Jesus' ministry not as curing people with health conditions, but as healing them in a transformative way. He said that in Jesus' day, people believed that health conditions were God's punishment for personal or ancestral sin. Consequently, those who had a health condition were regarded as being out of favor with God and were forced to live at the bottom of the social ladder, despairing over their situation in life and depending on others for their care. He believed that Jesus' charismatic preaching empowered people to transcend impairment caused by their health conditions and become productive members of society. At first, the professor's sweeping interpretation of the results of Jesus helping God with spiritual healing seemed reasonable to me. However, when I considered each healing reported in the Gospels from a medical perspective and in light of the ancient tradition of the Jews accurately documenting their oral history, I decided that the professor's interpretation of the spiritual healing in Jesus' ministry would apply to only a few of the people whom God healed with Jesus' help.

Also while I was in seminary, I had my field experience in pastoral ministry as the assistant minister of a church. After a Sunday worship service, during which I gave a sermon on prayer for healing, several people in the congregation told me that they or persons whom they knew had been healed of various health conditions through prayer. I subsequently commented to the senior minister how pleased I was to hear firsthand that prayer for healing works. Then, the minister told me a remarkable personal story of spiritual healing.

The minister said that early in his ministry he visited the home of a teenage daughter who was to have surgery for cancer of the brain the following day. After he parked his car in front of the home, he paused to think about what much needed words of comfort and hope he might give to the daughter and her family, which, he added, had recently experienced several tragic events and was facing the possibility of another as the daughter might soon die from the cancer. As the minister considered what to say when he visited the family, he suddenly experienced overwhelming compassion for it, burst into tears, and cried out, "God, please help them." Then he went into the home and prayed for the daughter and her family.

The following morning, the minster went to the hospital to be with the family during the daughter's operation, but when he arrived at the hospital's reception desk, he was told that operation had been cancelled after a pre-operative neurological evaluation and magnetic resonance imaging (MRI) of her brain showed that her brain cancer had "miraculously disappeared."

As I drove alone to the rehearsal for my graduation from the Chicago Theological Seminary in May of 1997, I wondered how I might best put my training and experience in ministry into use. A very clear inner voice replied, "You will work in healing ministry," and I immediately realized that I had at last received God's call to ministry! Soon thereafter, the seminary's dean invited me to teach a course bridging theology and medicine. This course included reviewing the history of spiritual healing in Christianity and developing spiritual healing services for various settings.

Thus began my healing ministry, which has since expanded to preaching and lecturing about spiritual healing in churches of several Protestant denominations and leading gatherings for spiritual healing in various church, hospital, home, and outdoor settings. I have also written several articles and two books[1,2] on spiritual healing.

Again, I wrote book to promote a broader awareness of our ability to help God heal us with ways that Jesus Christ used in spiritual healing. First, Dr. Busby provides a history of spiritual healing from pre-biblical times to now. Then, he describes Jesus' ways of engaging with God in spiritual healing and how they can be applied in a spiritual healing session. I also provide information on how to design and conduct a spiritual healing session, including its preparation and framework, and resources for it.

# B. HISTORY OF SPIRITUAL HEALING

## 1. In Pre-biblical and Old Testament Times

As described in the Holy Bible, the Jewish people lived for long periods of time in exile in Egypt and then Babylon, and subsequently with the Greeks and then the Romans who had occupied their land of Israel. Consequently, we might assume that the Jews would have adopted some of the dominant beliefs, especially of the more scientifically advanced Egyptians and Greeks, on the causes and treatment of various health conditions. However, this did not occur.

The Egyptians believed that human beings are born healthy, but are innately susceptible to many real and imaginary threats to their health, including intestinal putrefaction, demons, worms, insects, and poisonous breaths as a form of witchcraft.[3,4] Priest-physicians and lay physicians were taught that every major part of the human body had its own god, so they specialized in treating a particular organ or disease. Medical texts from ancient Egypt say that healthy people should receive noxious remedies to keep demons away, and sick people should receive purging and exorcism and list various drugs to clear the body of disease-causing agents. For many centuries, Egyptians with various health conditions visited a temple erected over the grave of Imhotep (ca. 2980 B.C.E.), who in life was a renowned physician, priest, architect, astronomer, and advisor to the pharaoh, and in death, became the Egyptian god of medicine. People with a health condition would sleep overnight on a cot in the temple, attended by priests who encouraged them to anticipate the appearance of Imhotep's spirit to heal their health condition. Treatment given in the temple included baths in "holy water," isolation, and "therapeutic dreams." In time, the Greeks and Romans adopted this temple care.

The Babylonians believed that health conditions were punishment for their sins by male and female gods, who allowed them to be attacked by disease-causing demons believed always swarming around them to invade their bodies[3,4] Consequently, Babylonian priests, physicians, and priest-physicians treated health conditions with exorcism and the ingestion of noxious substances to force demons from the body, animal sacrifice to appease the gods, and prophesy to determine the will of the gods. Eventually, the Babylonians began to go beyond their supernatural therapies with specific drugs

The Greeks and Romans connected their health conditions with fate or chance and, as their literature describes, with the gods' displeasure over matters usually beyond human control.[5] Medicine as an art, science, and profession was established in Greece by Hippocrates (c.460-c.361 B.C.E.), who became known as the "father of medicine." Hippocrates believed that a health condition was not the result of possession by demons or punishment by the gods but due to a natural process that could be treated by diet, drugs, or surgery.[3,4] However, the physicians who practiced in the Hippocratic tradition were not against calling upon the gods for help in healing. The Greeks, and to a lesser extent, the Romans, erected healing temples dedicated to various gods, particularly Asclepius, a Greek hero who was first mentioned in Homer's Iliad and later became the Greek god of medicine and healing. The care that the Greeks and Romans received in their healing temples was similar to the care that the Egyptians received in the Imhotep temple.

The early Jews had entirely different perceptions of what causes a health condition and how it should be treated. These perceptions stemmed from revelations made to them by their one-and-only God, and their limited understanding of the afterlife. They believed that

## WE CAN HELP GOD HEAL US

God had absolute control over their lives, and that their ethical and moral behavior, as viewed through the eyes of God, determined whether God would provide them with good things, including health, or bad things, including health conditions.[5,6] They also believed that God's goodness had to be experienced in this life, if at all, leading them to place high values on the rewards and punishments that they attributed to God.

The Old Testament of the Bible clearly defines God's control over health and health conditions by rewarding moral living with health and punishing sinful living with a health condition. God says in one passage: *I kill and I make alive; I wound and I heal; and no one can deliver from my hand* (Deut 32:39), and in another passage: *"If you will listen carefully to the voice of the LORD your God, and do what is right in his sight, and give heed to his commandments and keep all his statutes, I will not bring upon you any of the diseases that I brought upon the Egyptians; for I am the LORD who heals you"* (Ex 15:26). Initially, God proclaims that children will be punished with a health condition for sins committed by their ancestors: *"The LORD, the LORD, a God merciful and gracious, slow to anger, and abounding in steadfast love and faithfulness, keeping steadfast love for the thousandth generation, forgiving iniquity and transgression and sin, yet by no means clearing the guilty, but visiting the iniquity of the parents upon the children and the children's children, to the third and fourth generation"* (Ex 34: 6, 7). Later, God seems to have a change of mind on ancestral sin being the cause of a health condition: *In those days they shall no longer say: "The parents have eaten sour grapes, and the children's teeth are set on edge." But all shall die for their own sins; the teeth of everyone who eats sour grapes shall be set on edge* (Jer 31:29, 30).

Several prayers in the book of Psalms incorporate this divine reward-punishment system into them: *As for me, I said, "O LORD, be gracious to me; heal me, for I have sinned against you"* (Ps 41:4; see also 6:1, 2, 38:1-3 and 119:65-72). And other books of the Old Testament contain many accounts of God punishing large numbers of people and individuals with a health condition. God struck the Jews with two plagues because of their repeated unfaithfulness (Num 11:18-20, 31-33; 16:41-50), Miriam with leprosy because she spoke out against her brother, Moses (Num 12:1, 5-10), and the nation of Israel with a pestilence because David took a census of the fighting men (2 Sam 24:1, 15). Debatably unfair was God's punishment of a pharaoh and his household with great plagues because the pharaoh took Abram's wife, Sarai, to be his own after Abram passed her off as his sister (Gen 12:10-15, 17). Even a Jewish prophet could be an agent for the administration of divine punishment, such as when Elisha inflicted Naaman's leprosy upon his servant, Gehazi, for lying to him (2 Kings 5:25-27). Interestingly, the reward-punishment system of the Old Testament is challenged in the book of Job, which appears to have originated from an ancient folktale from Egypt or Babylon[7]. In it, a wealthy, righteous man called Job challenges God to show him what he has done wrong to deserve being punished by God with a terrible skin condition and other serious misfortunes.

The Old Testament gives little indication of Jews receiving treatment from physicians, evidently for the reason that secular healing practices would be working against the will of God in punishing sins with health conditions.[8] Moreover, the Old Testament contained numerous divinely prescribed rules (see Lev 11-16) that were directed much more at purifying than healing the body, consequently giving physicians a secondary role to priests in healing.[9] One Old Testament author suggests that as compared to God, Jewish physicians are worthless for healing in his description of King Asa's death: *In the thirty-ninth year of his reign Asa was diseased in his feet, and his disease became severe; yet even in his disease he did not seek the LORD, but sought help from physicians* (2 Chron 16:12). Much later, however, another author gives a favorable opinion of physicians:

*Honor physicians for their services, for the Lord created them; for their gift of healing comes from the Most High, and they are rewarded by the king. The skill of physicians makes them distinguished, and in the presence of the great they are admired* (Sir 38:1-3). But then this author falls back on tradition, acknowledging God as the source of healing of a health condition that is a divine punishment for sin: *My child, when you are ill, do not delay, but pray to the Lord, and he will heal you. Give up your faults and direct your hands rightly, and cleanse your heart from all sin* (Sir 38:9, 10). Here, one can see the influence of Greek medicine on the attitude of the Jews toward the practice of medicine. With physicians now being regarded as instruments in the hands of God, they were usually held blameless for errors on their part, whether or not the errors were due to negligence, thus leaving judgment of negligence and the administration of punishment for such errors to God.[10]

In contrast to the New Testament, accounts of spiritual healing were few in the Old Testament. Abimelech, his wife, and female slaves were healed when Abraham prayed for them (Gen 21:17). King Jeroboam's withered hand was restored when an unknown prophet prayed for him (1 Kings 13:6). A widow's dead son was revived when the prophet Elijah prayed for him and laid upon him (1 Kings 17:17-22), and a Shunamite woman's dead son was revived when the prophet Elisha did the same for him as Elijah did for the widow's dead son (2 Kings 4:32-35). The leprosy which was infecting Naaman, commander of the army of the king of Aram, cleared when, through a messenger, Elisha ordered him to go and wash himself seven times in the Jordan River (2 Kings 5:1, 10, 14). King Hezekiah recovered from a boil after he prayed to God to heal it (2 Kings 20:1-11).

Finally, the God of the Old Testament speaks through the prophets Isaiah and Malachi about coming to earth to heal. In an Isaiah oracle, God tells the Jews that when God comes to save them from their exile in Babylon: *Then the eyes of the blind shall be opened, and the ears of the deaf unstopped; then the lame shall leap like a deer, and the tongue of the speechless sing for joy* (Isa 35: 5, 6). One of Isaiah's so-called suffering servant songs describes the suffering that an unnamed "servant" who guides the Jews out of their exile in Babylon will have to endure: *He was despised and rejected by others; a man of suffering and acquainted with infirmity; and as one from whom others hide their faces he was despised, and we held him of no account. Surely he has borne out our infirmities and carried our diseases; yet we accounted him stricken, struck down by God, and afflicted. But he was wounded for our transgressions, crushed for our iniquities; upon him was the punishment that made us whole, and by his bruises we are healed* (Isa 53:3-5). Through Malachi, God said: *But for you who revere my name the sun of righteousness shall rise, with healing in its wings* (Mal 4:2). The Gospel writers, Matthew and Luke, would eventually link these Old Testament prophesies to Jesus Christ (see Mt 11:5 and Lk 7:22).

## 2. In New Testament Times

In the New Testament of the Holy Bible, we find that spiritual healing was a vital part of the ministry of Jesus Christ and that after his life on Earth, it continued in the ministries of his disciples and apostles mentioned in the Holy Bible. One-fifth of the entire Gospels describes thirty-nine separate occasions when Jesus Christ engaged in spiritual healing,[5] summarized in APPENDIX A.

Often when I lecture about the spiritual healing that is described in the New Testament, I am asked whether stories of spiritual healing by Jesus Christ and his followers could have been misunderstood or embellished as they were passed along by word of mouth in the years before the Gospels were written. My answer has always been that the first-century Jews had a very strong oral tradition, so we can assume that the essence of these stories stood the test of time until they were told in the Gospels.[11,12] And I add hat leprosy and demonic possession, mentioned quite frequently in the New Testament, could have been the names for health conditions that have different named than in the modern world.

The word "leprosy" is derived from the Greek word *lepra,* or an itchy, powdery, or scaly thickening of the skin. This word came into being about 800 B.C.E., when it was applied to true leprosy, a chronic, disfiguring bacterial infection involving primarily the skin.[13] It is also called Hansen's disease, named for the Norwegian physician who discovered its cause in 1873.[14] Ancient writings show that leprosy first appeared in India, and subsequently spread worldwide. As with many health conditions, leprosy was often considered divine punishment for worldly sins. Although leprosy is mentioned many times in the Gospels and only a few times in the Old Testament, it was not endemic in the biblical world.[13] Therefore, the word leprosy appears to have been used generically in translations of the Holy Bible not only to refer to the disease of leprosy, but also to various other skin conditions, such as psoriasis, eczema, seborrheic dermatitis, and severe fungus infection.[15]

The belief that a demon, or an evil or unclean spirit, could possess the human spirit and cause a health condition was prevalent among the Jews in biblical times.[10] This phenomenon is mentioned only twice in the Old Testament (see 1 Sam 16:14, 15, 23; Tob 6:8, 14; 8:2, 3) as compared to 12 times in the New Testament. Nothing in the Gospels indicates that Jesus believed in demonic possession, but he appears to have referred to "demon" or "demons" while attempting to convince people that he had effectively dealt with what the Jews believed was causing their various health conditions.[16] Undoubtedly, the Jews suffered from various neuropsychiatric disorders, which could have been provoked or aggravated by their belief in health conditions being God's punishment for sin, especially if they resulted in people being shunned by society.[8,15] Moreover, we are seeing increasingly credible evidence that the spirits of departed persons can attach themselves to the spirits of living persons and either cause a health condition or produce symptoms that mimic one [15,17,18,19]

Therefore, we might hypothesize that the demon-possessed persons described by the gospel writers could have been suffering either from neuropsychiatric disorders or spirit attachments, or even both.

The gospel accounts of spiritual healing attributed to Jesus Christ tell us that by restoring people with health conditions to physical, mental, emotional, and spiritual wholeness, he was concerned for the health of the whole person. He seemed to have compassion for everyone with a health condition whom he encountered. For example, the Gospel of Matthew says: *When he [Jesus] went ashore, he saw a great crowd; and he had compassion for them and cured their sick* (Mt 14:14). And later, Matthew's Gospel states: *As they [Jesus and his disciples] were leaving Jericho, a large crowd followed him. There were two blind men sitting by the roadside. When they heard that Jesus was passing by, they shouted, "Lord, have mercy upon us, Son of David!" ... Jesus stood still and called them, saying, "What do you want me to do for you?" They said to him, "Lord, let our eyes be opened." Moved with compassion, Jesus touched their eyes. Immediately they regained their sight and followed him* (Mt 20:29, 30, 32-34).

Jesus appears to have understood that most causes of health conditions during his time on Earth were beyond human control.[5] Moreover, he hesitates to speculate on possible causes, as John describes in his Gospel: *As he [Jesus] walked along, he saw a man blind from birth. His disciples asked him, "Rabbi, who sinned, this man or his parents, that he was born blind?" Jesus answered, "Neither he nor his parents sinned; he was born blind so that God's works might be revealed in him"* (Jn 9:1-3). Notably, this passage, combined with the fact that Jesus never asked a person with a health condition what sin that person or an ancestor had committed, appears to indicate that Jesus did not believe that God punishes personal or ancestral sin with a health condition.

Jesus cared so much about people that he made every effort to perform spiritual healing on as many persons who had health conditions as possible.[5] In his Gospel, Luke suggests that Jesus would minister to those with health conditions to the point of fatigue from loss of spiritual energy, which would be restored through prayer in private: *But now more than ever the word about Jesus spread abroad; many crowds would gather to hear him and to be cured of their diseases. But he would withdraw to deserted places and pray* (Lk 5:15, 16; see also Mt 14:23; Mk 6:46).

Luke describes Jesus' channeling, or receiving, conducting, and transmitting an energy for spiritual healing in a passage about a woman in a crowd, who was immediately healed of chronic gynecological bleeding after touching the fringe of Jesus' clothes: *Then Jesus asked, "Who touched me?" When all denied it, Peter said, "Master, the crowds surround you and press in on you." But Jesus said, "Someone touched me; for I noticed power had gone out from me." When the woman saw that she could not remain hidden, she came trembling; and falling down before him, she declared in the presence of all the people why she touched him, and how she had been immediately healed. He said to her, "Daughter, your faith has made you well; go in peace"* (Lk 8:45-48; see also Mt 9:20-22 and Mk 5:25-34). As I experience in my healing ministry, and have observed in others engaged in it, depletion of universal vital life force energy in the body by the repeated or prolonged channeling of the energy can produce a physical, mental, emotional, and spiritual fatigue that calls for a period of rest, prayer, or meditation for energy renewal.

Jesus used divine healing energy to heal persons with whom he was in direct contact, or direct healing, and persons who were at some distance from him, or distant spiritual healing. Mark describes the direct healing of a man's deafness and speech impediment: *They brought to him a deaf man who had an impediment in his speech; and they begged him to lay his hand on him. He took him aside in private, away from the crowd, and put his fingers into his ears, and he spat and touched his tongue. Then looking up to heaven, he sighed and said to him, "Ephphatha," that is, "Be opened." And immediately his ears were opened, his tongue was released, and he spoke plainly* (Mk 7:32-35). John describes distantt healing of a royal official's son: *Now there was a royal official whose son lay ill in Capernaum. When he heard* that Jesus had come from Judea to Galilee, he went and begged him to come down and heal his son, for he was at the point of death. Then Jesus said to him, "Unless you see signs and wonders you will not believe." The official said to him, "Sir, come down before my little boy dies." Jesus said to him, "Go; your son will live." The man believed the word that Jesus spoke to him and started on his way. As he was going down, his slaves met him and told him that his child was alive. So he asked them the hour when he began to recover, and they said to him, "Yesterday at one in the afternoon the fever left him." The father realized that this was the hour when Jesus had said to him, "Your son will live " So he himself believed, along with his whole household (Jn 4:46-53; see also Mt 8:5-13 and Lk 7:1-10).

Jesus made his healing ministry available to all people, at all times and in all places.[20] He provided spiritual healing to many persons who were off limits to Jewish piety, including ritually unclean persons such as lepers and Gentiles. Mark says, *A leper came to him begging him* [Jesus], *and kneeling he said to him, "If you choose, you can make me clean." Moved with pity, Jesus stretched out his hand and touched him, and said to him, "I do choose. Be made clean!" Immediately the leprosy left him, and he was made clean* (Mk 1:40-42; see also Mt 8:2, 3 and Lk 5:12-13). Matthew says, *Just then a Canaanite woman from that region came out and started shouting, "Have mercy on me, Lord, Son of David* [Jesus]; *my daughter is tormented by a demon." But he did not answer her at all. And his disciples came and urged him, saying, "Send her away, for she keeps shouting after us." He answered, "I was sent only to the lost sheep of the house of Israel." But she came and knelt before him, saying, "Lord, help me." He answered, "It is not fair to take the children's food and throw it to the dogs." She said, "Yes, Lord, yet even the dogs eat the crumbs that fall from their masters' table." Then Jesus answered her, "Woman, great is your faith! Let it be done for you as you wish." And her daughter was healed instantly* (Mt 15:22-28; see also Mk 7:24-30). And to the chagrin of the religious elite, Jesus engaged in spiritual healing on the Sabbath, even in a synagogue, as Luke wrote: *On another Sabbath he* [Jesus] *entered the synagogue and taught, and there was a man there whose right hand was withered. The scribes and the Pharisees watched him to see whether he would cure on the Sabbath, so that they might find an accusation against him. Even though he knew what they were thinking, he said to the man who had the withered hand, "Come and stand here." He got up and stood there. Then Jesus said to them, "I ask you, is it lawful to do good or to do harm on the Sabbath, to save life or destroy it?" After looking around at all of them, he said to him, "Stretch out your hand." He did so, and his hand was restored* (Lk 6:6-10; see also Mt 12:9-13 and Mk 3:1-5).

While engaged in spiritual healing, Jesus often used words, touch, or both, and occasionally saliva. His words for healing were usually spoken as commands. His touch for healing, as well as gospel descriptions of people being healed when they touched him, show that he was a remarkable conduit for divine healing energy. Use of his own saliva for healing blindness appears to reflect the prevailing Jewish belief that saliva, especially from a prominent person, can cure eye problems.[10]

Jesus' use of prayer in addition to commanding words for healing seems likely. He told his disciples that prayer was necessary to exorcise a certain kind of demon, as Mark describes when Jesus' disciples failed to cure a boy with a demon: *When Jesus saw that a crowd came running together, he rebuked the unclean spirit, saying to it, "You spirit that keep this boy from speaking and hearing, I command you, come out of him, and never enter him again!" After crying out and convulsing him terribly, it came out, and the boy was like a corpse, so that most of them said, "He is dead." But Jesus took him by the hand and lifted him up, and he was able to stand. When he had entered the house, his disciples asked him privately, "Why could we not cast it out?" He said to them, "This kind can come out only through prayer"* (Mk 9:25-29). Jesus also assured his disciples that their prayers would be answered. He was quoted by Matthew as saying that one must pray with faith: *"Whatever you ask for in prayer with faith, you will receive"* (Mt 21:22). And he was quoted by Mark as saying that one must pray with belief in the prayer already having been answered: *"So I tell you, whatever you ask for in prayer, believe that you have received it, and it will be yours"* (Mk 11:24). John provides three quotes of Jesus indicating that a favorable response to asking for something in prayer if his name is used in the asking: *"I will do whatever you ask in my name, so that the Father may be glorified in his Son. If in my name you ask me for anything, I will do it"* (Jn 14:13, 14), *"If you abide in me, and my words abide in you, ask for whatever you wish, and it will be done for you"* (Jn 15:7), and, *"Very truly, I tell you, if you ask anything of the Father in my name, he will give it to you"* (Jn 16:23). Notably, "In my name" in Aramaic, the language Jesus spoke, means "as I would do it."[21] So when we add "in Jesus' name" or a similar phrase to a prayer, we are taking on the personality of Jesus and praying as Jesus would have prayed.[22] Although some may assume that to say "in Jesus' name" in a prayer gives greater weight to the prayer, I believe this is not what Jesus intended in recommending the use of "in my (Jesus') name" in prayers.

Jesus related faith to his spiritual healing on several occasions. As described above, he told the woman who was healed of a longstanding issue of blood that her faith had made her well (Lk 8:48). Also, he told the Canaanite woman that she had great faith in asking him to heal her daughter of a tormenting demon (Mt 15:28). Matthew quotes Jesus saying to two men as he was healing them of blindness, *"According to your faith let it be done to you"* (Mt 9:29); Mark quotes Jesus saying to Bartimaeus whom he had just healed of blindness: *"Go: your faith has made you well"* (Mk 10:46-52). Luke quotes Jesus saying to one man whom he had healed of leprosy and another man whom he had healed of blindness: *"your faith has made you well"* (Lk 17:12; 18:35-43). Matthew, Mark and Luke report that Jesus saw *"faith"* in the friends of a paralyzed man who carried the man on his bed to Jesus for healing (Mt 9:2; Mk 2:3-5, 10-12; Lk 5:17-26). Matthew says that when a Roman centurion respectfully asked Jesus to heal his servant, who was paralyzed and in terrible distress at home, Jesus said: *"Go: let it be done for you according to your faith"*

# WE CAN HELP GOD HEAL US

(Mt 8:5-13; see also Lk 7:2-10). We might ask whether Jesus' use of the word, "faith," when he performed spiritual healing meant faith in his ability to perform spiritual healing or faith in God. Since Jesus was so strongly focused on awakening the people's spirits to become connected to divine healing energy,[5] I have no doubt that he was referring to faith in God, or "spiritual faith" (see Chapter C.1.).

Whenever I preach or teach about spiritual healing, or speak at a session for spiritual healing, I make a statement about Jesus' healing ministry, to which many listeners have responded with looks of surprise or relief, and sometimes with tears. I say that Jesus never asked a person who came to him for spiritual healing what sin he or she, or even an ancestor, had committed to deserve God's punishment for it with any sort of health condition. I also say that Jesus even told his disciples that he did not believe that God punishes sin with a health condition, as John wrote in his Gospel: *As he [Jesus] walked along, he saw a man blind from birth. His disciples asked him, "Rabbi, who sinned, this man or his parents, that he was born blind?" Jesus answered, "Neither this man nor his parents sinned; he was born blind so that God's works might be revealed in him"* (Jn 9:1-3). But I have been ready to explain why Jesus appeared to link sin with health conditions in two accounts of his engaging in spiritual healing. First, Mark wrote that Jesus forgave the sins of a man after healing his paralysis not by acknowledging that his paralysis was due to sin, but by assuring the man that forgiveness, as well as healing, comes from God: *And when they could not bring him* [a paralyzed man] *to Jesus because of the crowd, they removed the roof above him; and after having dug through it, they let down the mat on which the paralytic lay. When Jesus saw their faith, he said to the paralytic, "Son, your sins are forgiven"* (Mk 2:4, 5). Second, John wrote that Jesus helped God to cure a man's infirmity, and then told the man that he had sinned by exaggerating the severity of the infirmity rather than his infirmity being God's punishment for sin: *Now in Jerusalem by the Sheep Gate there is a pool, called in Hebrew Beth-zatha, which has five porticoes. In these lay many invalids — blind, lame, and paralyzed. One man was*

19

there who had been ill for thirty-eight years. When Jesus saw him lying there and knew that he had been there a long time, he said to him, "Do you want to be made well?" The sick man answered him, "Sir, I have no one to put me into the pool when the water is stirred up; and while I am making my way, someone else steps down ahead of me." Jesus said to him, "Stand up, take your mat and walk." At once the man was made well, and he took up his mat and began to walk. ... Later Jesus found him in the temple and said to him, "See, you have been made well! Do not sin any more, so that nothing worse happens to you" (Jn 5:2-9, 14).

We might wonder why spiritual healing was so much a part of Jesus' ministry, when Jesus was such an extraordinarily charismatic teacher and preacher of the Word of God.[6] On the one hand, we might presume that Jesus healed simply because he was a specially gifted and remarkably compassionate spiritual healer. On the other hand, we might presume he used spiritual healing for one or more definitive purposes, such as confirming his coming as the Messiah, validating the gospel message, demonstrating the arrival of God's realm on earth, energizing people's faith in God, bringing people to repentance, and even establishing the Church.[6,15,23] All of these presumptions seem plausible to me, but none of them take into account the fundamental question of why God has made universal vital life force energy available to all human beings for healing. I believe the answer becomes clear when we look at what Jesus embodied in his ministry: God's unconditional love for us, in wanting us to be whole - physically, mentally, emotionally, and spiritually.

Mark describes how Jesus empowered his disciples and sent them on a ministry that included spiritual healing: *He [Jesus] called the twelve and began to send them out two by two, and gave them authority over unclean spirits. ... So they went out and proclaimed that all should repent. They cast out many demons, and anointed with oil many who were sick and cured them* (Mk 6:7, 12, 13; see also Mt 10:1, 5-8 and Lk 9:1, 2, 6). [Anointing with oil, or unction, is an ancient religious ritual for healing.] Luke reports that many spoke to Jesus

## WE CAN HELP GOD HEAL US

about becoming engaged in his ministry, and: *After this the Lord [Jesus] appointed seventy others and sent them on ahead of him in pairs to every town and place where he himself intended to go* (Lk 10:1). He also told them that: *"Whenever you enter a town and its people welcome you, eat what is set before you; cure the sick who are there"* (Lk 10:8, 9). The longer ending of the Mark's Gospel says that Jesus appeared to his disciples just before his Ascension and: *He said to them, "Go into all the world and proclaim the good news to the whole creation. ... And these signs will accompany those who believe; by using my name they will cast out demons; ... they will lay their hands on the sick, and they will recover"* (Mk 16:15, 17, 18). So the spiritual healing which was very much a part of Jesus' ministry, continued.

In his book of Acts, Luke wrote that after the Pentecost, or descent of the Holy Spirit upon the disciples, apostles and other followers of Jesus Christ after his Ascension, the apostles and new disciples performed *"signs and wonders"* among the people, indicating that possibly all of them were engaged in spiritual healing (see Acts 2:43; 5:12; 6:8; 8:13; 14:3; 15:12). In his Book of Acts, Luke described thirteen separate occasions when the apostles and new disciples became engaged in spiritual healing, summarized in APPENDIX B.

As in Jesus' healing ministry, the apostles and disciples used words, touch, or both, on most occasions for spiritual healing. Although Jesus had told his disciples to pray for healing, prayer was reportedly used on only two occasions. On one occasion Peter raised Tabitha: *Now in Joppa there was a disciple whose name was Tabitha, which in Greek is Dorcas. She was devoted to good works and acts of charity. At that time she became ill and died. ... Since Lydda was near Joppa, the disciples, who heard that Peter was there, sent two men to him with the request, "Please come to us without delay." So Peter got up and went with them; ... and when he arrived, they took him to the room upstairs. ... Peter put all of them outside, and then he knelt down and prayed. He turned to the body and said, "Tabitha, get up." Then she opened her eyes, and seeing Peter, she sat up* (Acts 9:36, 37, 38, 39, 40). On the other occasion, Paul healed the father of Publius, the Governor of Malta: *It so happened that the father of Publius lay sick in bed with fever and dysentery. Paul visited him and cured him by praying and putting his hands on him* (Acts 28:8). Finally, faith is mentioned only once as having been observed by Paul in a person who received spiritual healing through Paul: *In Lystra there was a man sitting who could not use his feet and had never walked, for he had been crippled from birth. He listened to Paul as he was speaking. And Paul, looking at him intently and seeing that he had faith to be healed, said in a loud voice, "Stand upright on your feet." And the man sprang up and began to walk* (Acts 14:8-10).

Unfortunately, Jesus' teaching did not erase belief in health conditions being God's punishment for sin, as we read in Acts, Paul's letters to the Corinthians, and the anonymous letter to the Hebrews. Ananias and then his wife Sapphira, suddenly died when confronted by Peter for lying about sharing all of their possessions with the others in the early Church (Acts 5:1-10). The Jewish sorcerer Bar-Jesus (Elymas), who was opposed to teaching about Jesus Christ, became blind, as Paul predicted (Acts 13:6-12). Paul wrote to the Corinthians that the reason for many of them being weak and sick was the unworthy manner in which they had participated in the Lord's Supper (1 Cor 11:27-33). Paul also said that God has sent him an affliction (*"thorn"*) of some sort to keep him humble (2 Cor 12:7-10). The letter to the Hebrews reiterates an Old Testament proverb (Prov 3:11, 12): *And you have forgotten the exhortation that addresses you as children* — *"My child, do not regard lightly the discipline of the Lord, or lose heart when you are punished by him; for the Lord disciplines those whom he loves, and chastises every child whom he accepts"* (Heb 12:5, 6). Finally, the letter of James suggests that this belief still existed in early Christian communities, when James says that while their elders, or leaders are praying for those who need healing: ... *anyone who has committed sins will be forgiven* (Jas 5:15).

Except in the Letter of James, no other description or mention is subsequently made of spiritual healing in the New Testament. In his letter to the early Church at Corinth, Paul said that certain people are uniquely capable of helping God with spiritual healing as one of several special gifts from God to humanity: *To one is given through the Spirit the utterance of wisdom, and to another the utterance of knowledge according to the same Spirit to another faith by the same Spirit, to another gifts of healing by the one Spirit, to another the working of miracles, to another prophecy, to another the discernment of spirits, to another various kinds of tongues, to another the interpretation of tongues* (1 Cor 12:8-10). However, he also wrote that everyone receives these gifts, which would include spiritual healing, albeit the capacity to use individual gifts is much greater in some people than in others: *Now there are varieties of gifts, but the same Spirit and there are varieties of services, but the same Lord; and there are varieties of activities, but it is the same God who activates all of them in everyone. ... All these are activated by one and the same Spirit, who allots to each one individually just as the Spirit chooses* (1 Cor 12:4-6, 11).

In the letter of James, the historical record of spiritual healing in the New Testament closes with instructions on how spiritual healing is to be performed. As I will describe in Chapter B.3., a subsequent mistranslation of a key word [from "heal" to "sick," as in the NRSV Holy Bible quotation below] in the original instructions had a negative impact on spiritual healing within the Western Church for many centuries. James wrote: *Are any among you sick? They should call for the elders of the church and have them pray over them, anointing them with oil* [unction] *in the name of the Lord. The prayer of faith will save* [originally "heal"] *the sick, and the Lord will raise them up; and anyone who has committed sins will be forgiven. Therefore confess your sins to one another, and pray for one another, so that you may be healed. The prayer of the righteous is powerful and effective* (Jas 5:14-16).

James' letter suggests that principally the elders of the Early Church were engaged in spiritual healing, as opposed to larger gatherings of devout Christians. Therefore, we can presume from what Paul said about some people having the special gift for spiritual healing, that most, if not all, of the elders to whom James was referring possessed this gift.

The book of Acts, the letters of Paul to the Corinthians and the letter of James indicate that the disciples, apostles, and elders performed only direct spiritual healing, using prayer in Jesus' name, the laying on of hands, and unction as Jesus had directed his disciples to do. Again, when Jesus asked that prayer for healing be done in his name, he was saying in Aramaic, the language he spoke, "as I would do it."[21]

## 3. From Biblical Times to the Present

From the writings of the early Church, we learn that spiritual healing remained very much a part of its ministry as Christians shared their conviction that their God was both a loving and healing presence in their lives.[5] Deacons were designated to serve people with health conditions and to give their names to their respective bishops who would pray for them.[24] Numerous spiritual healing events were described by great theologians of the time, including Justin Martyr (c.100-c.165 C.E.), Irenaeus (c.130-c.202. C.E.), Tertullian (c.160-c.220 C.E.), Origen (c.185-c.254 C.E.), Athanasius (c.296-373 C.E.), Basil the Great (c.329-379 C.E.) and John Chrysostom (c.345-407 C.E.).[5] Early spiritual healing practices included one or more of prayer, the laying on of hands, unction, exorcism, making the sign of the cross and, in time, communion as a routinely administered sacrament.

In the early years of the unified, formalized Church, persons could enter the priesthood without being ordained for it simply by saying that they had received God's special gift for spiritual healing.[5] Soon, however, the Church began to require that ordination be preceded by demonstrating this gift. Eventually, God was simply asked in prayer to grant the gift to the person being ordained. So over the years, God's special gift for spiritual healing, as had been described by Paul, was being absorbed into the priestly office, to be sought through ordination and used along with the sacraments.

The practice of spiritual healing has continued to this day in the Eastern (Orthodox) Church. However, it gradually faded and eventually ceased for over 400 years in the Western (eventually Roman Catholic) Church, apparently due to a mistranslation by Jerome. (c340-420 C.E.), a Latin Catholic priest, when he converted the much of the original Holy Bible from Greek into Latin. The Greek words for "heal" and "cure" in James 5:15 became *salvo* (save), rather than *sano* (heal) or *curo* (cure), in Jerome's Latin (Vulgate) Bible.[5,6] This mistranslation appears to have been the starting point for prayer, the laying on of hands and unction increasingly being used by the Roman Catholic Church as a sacrament for the "saving of souls" rather than for the "healing of bodies."*

Evidently fueling this sacramental shift from the healing of bodies to the saving of soul were statements made by three great theologians of the Western Church. Augustine (354-430 C.E.), Bishop of Hippo, said that sickness was sent by God to purify souls.[6] Pope Gregory the Great (540-604 C.E.) said that sickness was discipline from God to bring people to repentance.[5] Thomas Aquinas (1225-1274) said that Jesus came to earth especially to save souls and that the purpose of his spiritual healing was to demonstrate divine power to people so that they could believe in his teaching. And adding to the negativity towards prayer, the laying on of hands and unction for spiritual

---

* The mistranslation remained in the King James, Revised Standard, New Revised Standard and New Jerusalem versions of the Holy Bible, but was corrected in the New International and Contemporary English versions of the Holy Bible.

healing, at least in the formal setting of the Church, was a series of disastrous epidemics, especially the Black Death (bubonic and pneumonic plague) of 1348, which the incumbent pope, Nicholas V (1397-1455), declared was a punishment from God.[5,6]

Finally, the Council of Trent of the Roman Catholic Church declared in 1551 that the sacrament of "anointing is to be given to the sick, especially those who are in such a serious condition as to appear to have reached the end of their life. For this reason it is also called the sacrament of dying."[25] This sacrament of dying would soon become known as "extreme unction," or "final anointing."

In 1962, the Vatican Council II amended the declaration of the Council of Trent by adding, "Extreme unction, which may also and more properly be called 'anointing of the sick,' is not a sacrament for those only who are at the point of death. Hence, as soon as any one of the faithful begins to be in danger of death from sickness or old age, the fitting time for that person to receive this sacrament has certainly already arrived."[25] Vatican II also added, "By the sacred anointing of the sick and the prayer of the presbyters, the whole Church commends the sick to the suffering of the glorified Lord so that he may raise them up and save them (see also Jas 5:14-15)."[25] In spite of these amendments, the Roman Catholic Church has apparently still not accepted the fact of Jerome's mistranslation.

Prior to the thirteenth century, physicians worked with priests in the Roman Catholic Church in attending to the physical, mental, emotional, and spiritual needs of persons with health conditions. In fact, priests could also practice medicine until banned from doing so by the church's Council of Tours in 1163.[5] Unfortunately, the religious philosophy espoused by Thomas Aquinas challenged this holistic approach to caring for persons with health conditions.

Aquinas adopted a teaching of the Greek philosopher, Aristotle, who said that humanity experiences only the natural world, whereas God exists in the realm of the supernatural and therefore can be experienced only through the use of reason. Aquinas also believed that further communication from God was essentially unnecessary

## WE CAN HELP GOD HEAL US

after Jesus' supernatural ministry. Putting these religious philosophies together, Aquinas wrote that any divine communication comes to us intellectually, or through some sensory or physical medium, so that gifts of the Spirit are no longer necessary.[5]

The Roman Catholic Church embraced Aquinas' perspective on the supremacy of rational thought for knowing God.[6] Then the philosopher, physicist and mathematician, René Descartes (1596-1650), took this perspective a step further. He theorized that our reality is made up of parallel and equal worlds – one material (e.g., our body), and the other immaterial (e.g., our mental and spiritual selves) – which are separate from each other.[6] This theory, known as Cartesian dualism, paved the way for the separation of religion and science in the Enlightenment (1715-1799), an intellectual movement in Europe that questioned traditional beliefs, especially in religion, and emphasized the primacy of reason and the scientific method. So we find that an intellectual wall was erected between medicine and religion - a wall that has only recently started to come down.

Luther (1483-1546) and Calvin (1509-1564), the great Protestant reformers, echoed Aquinas in expressing their beliefs on the reality of spiritual healing.[5] Luther wrote that God dispensed the gifts of the Spirit, including spiritual healing, only to early Christians, so that the church could do greater works, such as teaching, converting people to Christianity, and saving souls. However, he appears to have accepted the reality of spiritual healing late in his life. Calvin wrote that gifts of the Spirit were given only in the beginning to make preaching of the Gospel wonderful. However, his later writings suggest that he might have begun to accept the reality of spiritual healing.

The Protestant churches in Europe and Great Britain continued to teach that God imposed health conditions as punishment for sin. However, they did not adopt the Roman Catholic sacrament of extreme unction. Some Protestant churches re-instituted spiritual healing, but gatherings for healing centered on confession of sin as the presumed cause of a health condition, in the hope that God would be merciful and send healing.

Since the days of the Christian martyrs in the First Century, spiritual healing has been occurring at shrines erected to various martyrs and other "saints" of the Church and at sites of reported apparitions, particularly of Mary, the mother of Jesus. The Roman Catholic Church, which has witnessed most of this spiritual healing down through the centuries, has never formally explained it or accepted the reality of it. However, common people in the Roman Catholic Church have always believed that in these sacred places, heavenly beings, or "saints," show what God's grace can do in their earthly lives, by praying along with them for spiritual healing.

Gregory of Nyssa (c.335-c.394 C.E.), brother of Basil the Great, wrote about spiritual healing at the Shrine of the Forty Martyrs, and John Chrysostom (c. 349–407 C.E.), Archbishop of Constantinople, of healing at the Shrine of St. Babylas the Martyr.[5] Gregory (c.538-594 C.E.), Bishop of Tours, wrote about spiritual healing at the Shrine of St. Martin of Tours, and mentioned that sleeping in shrines of martyrs and saints was being practiced quite frequently.[5] Currently, we have many shrines where spiritual healing is occurring, including the Shrine of Lourdes in France, the Shrine of Fatima in Portugal, the Shrine of Knock in Ireland, and the Martyrs Shrine in Canada.

We might wonder whether the healing that occurs at Christian shrines is due to a "placebo effect."* In recent years, the medical profession has proven that many people with serious health conditions who have visited these shrines have experienced cures that have defied known probabilities for the spontaneous remission of these conditions.[26,27] The intense spiritual energy in the shrines that I have visited along the remarkable spontaneous healing in them have led me to believe that spiritual healing in the shrines is truly authentic.

After biblical times, numerous Christians have had the divine special gift for spiritual healing. Most have discovered this gift while devoting their lives to caring for the sick and poor, while teaching and

---

*The beneficial effect of believing an inert substance or treatment has therapeutic value.

## WE CAN HELP GOD HEAL US

preaching the Word of God, or simply while having compassion for those with health conditions. Historically prominent spiritual healers have included Hilarion (c.291-c.371 C.E.), Martin of Tours (c.330-c.397 C.E.), Augustine of Canterbury (died c.604 C.E.), Francis of Assisi (1181-1226), Catherine of Siena (1347-1380), Ignatius of Loyola (c.1491-1556), Francis Xavier (1506-1552), George Fox (1624-1691), and John Wesley (1703-1791).[5] In the mid-1800's, Pastor Johann Christoph Blumhart baffled the Protestant church in Germany with remarkable spiritual healing in his ministry.[28]

In the past century, many individuals involved in the Pentecostal movement have discovered that they have God's special gift for spiritual healing, including Kathryn Kuhlman (1907-1976),[29] William Branham (1909-1965),[30] and Oral Roberts (1918-2009).[31] Specially gifted healers outside of this movement have included Joel Goldsmith (1892-1964)[32] who was a Christian mystic, Agnes Sanford (1897-1992),[33,34] who was the daughter of a Presbyterian missionary and the wife of an Episcopal priest, and Ambrose Worrall (1906-1972), who was assisted by his psychic wife, Olga (1906-1985).[35] More recently, Francis MacNutt (1925-2020)[36] and Ron Roth (1937-2009),[22,37] who initially discovered their special gifts for spiritual healing while serving as priests in the Roman Catholic Church, had highly successful spiritual healing ministries.

Very little has been written on the effectiveness of spiritual healing involving or not involving specially gifted healers, in spite of an "astonishing body of evidence all pointing in the direction of an extraordinary [healing] power being present."[36] The Worralls estimated that of numerous people who came to them for spiritual healing, about 90 per cent of people were "aided," and 50 to 60 percent of them were "made well."[35] MacNutt stated that in his large spiritual healing ministry, "The number of healings that take place seems well beyond the realm of chance occurrences," with about 25 per cent of people who desire spiritual healing being "cured," and 50 to 60 percent of them being "improved."[36] Notably, the Worralls and MacNutt suggested that if a single spiritual healing session has been ineffective, the session should be repeated one or more times a week for up to several weeks.[35,36] MacNutt has also suggested that if a spiritual healing session is for a chronic or severe health condition, the initial or subsequent sessions should be extended to one or more hours, as so-called "soaking prayer."[36] Finally, the Worralls and MacNutt have proposed that in certain situations, such as a high risk of the return of a health condition, a spiritual healing session should be repeated one or more times a week for up to several weeks to sustain the healing of the condition.[35,36]

The belief that God inflicts health conditions for sin and other misdeeds passed from the Roman Catholic to the Protestant Church, as reflected in *Book of Common Prayer* of the Church of England (Anglican Church), written in 1549 and officially published in 1662.[38] My quotes from it and its current successor are italicized. Its worship service for the healing of an individual, called the "Order for the Visitation of the Sick," begins with the minister urging the person with a health condition to understand that God is responsible for his or her suffering: *Wherefore, whatsoever your sickness is, know you certainly, that it is God's visitation. And for what cause soever this sickness is sent unto you; whether it be to try your patience for the example of others, and that your faith may be found in the day of the Lord, laudable, glorious, and honourable, to the increase of glory and endless felicity; or else it be sent unto you to correct and amend in you whatever doth offend the eyes of the your heavenly Father; know you certainly, that if you truly repent you of your sins, and bear your sickness patiently, trusting in God's mercy, for his dear Son Jesus Christ's sake, and render unto him humble thanks for his Fatherly visitation, submitting yourself wholly unto his will; it shall turn to your profit, and help you forward in the right way that leadeth unto everlasting life.* After the minister has the person acknowledge his or her belief in the articles of faith of the Anglican Church and repent for his or her sins, he forgives the sins and asks God to heal the person if it be God's will: *Almighty, everliving God, Maker of mankind, who dost correct those whom thou dost love, and chastise every one whom thou dost receive; We beseech thee to have mercy upon this thy servant visited with thine hand, and to grant that he may take his sickness patiently, and recover his bodily health (if it be thy gracious will); and whensoever his soul shall depart from the body, it may be without spot presented unto thee, through Jesus Christ our Lord. Amen.*

The *Book of Common Prayer* has been used by Anglican churches around the world and as a resource by other Protestant denominations in developing their books of worship services. In its latest American version, published by the Episcopal Church in 1976,[39] the "Order for the Visitation of the Sick" has evolved into a service called "Ministration to the Sick." This spiritual healing service for one or more persons no longer points to God as the cause of health conditions. However, it alludes to this possibility by placing repentance and forgiveness of sins before prayers for healing either as a special confession "if the sick person's conscience is troubled" or as a general confession. Moreover, if unction is to be performed, the minister will bless the oil with: *O Lord, holy Father, giver of health and salvation: Send your Holy Spirit to sanctify this oil; that, as your holy apostles anointed many that were sick and healed them, so may those who in faith and repentance receive this holy unction be made whole, through Jesus Christ our Lord, who lives and reigns with you and the Holy Spirit, one God, for ever and ever. Amen.* This prayer is followed by an anthem, with the minister singing, *Savior of the world, by your cross and precious blood you have redeemed us*, and the people responding, *Save us, and help us, we humbly beseech you, O Lord.* Subsequently, repentance and forgiveness of sins are not mentioned in either of two prayers for healing and an anointing prayer. However, after the anointing prayer, the minister may add forgiveness of sins: *As you are outwardly anointed with this holy oil, so may our heavenly Father grant you the inward anointing of the Holy Spirit. Of his great mercy, may he forgive you your sins, release you from suffering, and restore you to wholeness and strength. May he deliver you from all evil, preserve you in all goodness, and bring you to everlasting life, through Jesus Christ our Lord. Amen.*

I have given much thought to whether repentance and forgiveness of sins should be included in a spiritual healing session. I have concluded that repentance and forgiveness of sins could support or generate belief in a health condition being God's punishment for a sin or sins, and consequently hamper the process of spiritual healing and even other forms of our healing. Rather than including repentance and forgiveness of sins in a spiritual healing session, I recommend that early in a spiritual healing session, I suggest that its leader mention that this belief is still of great concern to many people who are suffering from a serious health condition, and that they can be comforted by the fact that Jesus never stated that a health condition could be God's punishment for sin.

In summary, history has shown that God makes spiritual healing possible for us when we channel, or receive, conduct, and transmit, universal vital life force energy, or the healing energy of the Holy Spirit, to help God heal us. It has also shown that God has given some people a special gift and all others a natural gift to channel this energy.

Jesus Christ showed his followers how to engage in direct and distant spiritual healing - a divine legacy which has been successfully followed by Christians since he lived on Earth. Specifically, he demonstrated that essential to channeling this energy effectively are spiritual faith, compassion, prayer, and for direct spiritual healing, touch as the laying on of hands. In contrast to what has subsequently occurred in the Church's practice of spiritual healing, Jesus did not believe that health conditions are God's punishment for sin as implied by including repentance and forgiveness in its services for spiritual healing, or that the conduct of spiritual healing should be limited its clergy and other worship leaders, or that spiritual healing should be sacramental in its liturgy and practice. I believe that just as Jesus engaged in spiritual healing on anyone who asked for it, he would expect us to use his ways of spiritual healing, unaltered by the Church, in healing sessions which are held for us to actually help God with spiritual healing. I reflect this throughout the remainder of the book.

## C. JESUS' WAYS FOR SPIRITUAL HEALING

As I described in Chapter B.2., Jesus Christ engaged in direct and distant spiritual healing by channeling the healing energy coming from God. The ways that he did this involved spiritual faith, compassion, prayer, and for direct healing, touch as the laying on of hands. In this chapter, each is considered in light of our being able to help God heal us.

### 1. Spiritual Faith

"Spiritual faith," along with compassion, substantially participates in opening our spirits and energizing the intentionality of our praying to be channels for the healing energy of the God's Spirit. It encompasses both a firm belief and an absolute trust in God. The apostle Paul wrote that it is a gracious gift from God to all of us (1 Cor 12:4-6, 9).

Spiritual faith is described in the story of "The Healing of Blind Bartimaeus" by Jesus. Bartimaeus was a blind beggar who seems to have known that Jesus was engaged in spiritual healing. He was sitting by a roadside when he heard that Jesus was passing by in a large crowd, and he had to call out repeatedly to Jesus with an increasingly loud voice to ask Jesus for the healing of his blindness. Bartimaeus eventually got Jesus' attention. Jesus said to him: *"What do you want me to do for you?" The blind man said to him, "My teacher, let me see again." Jesus said to him, "Go; your faith has made you well." Immediately he regained his sight and followed him on the way* (Mk 10:51, 52).

What makes having spiritual faith possible? Several years ago, cardiologist Herbert Benson, a well-known pioneer in "mind-body" (psychosomatic) medicine and one of the first Western physicians to bring spirituality and healing into medicine, suggested that our chromosomes might have a "God gene" for spiritual faith.[40] Subsequently, visionary Gregg Braden proposed that our spiritual faith comes from Yahweh, the Hebrew name for God, being coded into our genetic structure.[41]

Do we really need to have a physical entity, such as a gene, to make our connection with God, and consequently be responsible for our spiritual faith? In contrast to what Benson and Braden have said about such a God connection, I believe that spiritual faith stems from the spiritual relationship that our pre-existing, inborn spirit continues to have with God during our mortal life. This relationship would responsible for our becoming aware of God's presence in our lives, or as Albert Einstein said, for his becoming aware of a "superior intelligence" in his life.[42,43] With maturation of our spirituality and our experiences of the divine, this awareness forms our spiritual faith – the faith that provides increasing intentionality to our prayer, such as for spiritual healing

Spiritual faith must be distinguished from two other types of faith: "medical faith" and "religious faith." Both of them are associated with positive mental and emotional states that are known to have beneficial effects on preserving health and promoting healing, principally through stimulation of the body's immune system.[44] A positive mental state would include belief, trust, intent, and confidence, and a positive emotional state would include optimism, hope, joy, and peace.

We have learned much about the role of medical faith in healing from the field of mind-body (psychosomatic) medicine, which began to develop in the mid 1900's.[45] Medical researchers have found that a patient's strong confidence in the medical care of her or his health condition, especially when coupled with an intense desire to recover from the condition, can greatly enhance the healing process.[40,45,46] They have also found that prescribing a placebo, or harmless drug, can have the same healing effect when the patient strongly believes that it will be effective for his or her health condition. Such findings in research on medical faith in healing led to creation of the medical science of psychoneuroimmunology.

We would expect that religious faith, particularly in the form of expectant trust in God's promises, should benefit people with various health conditions much like medical faith, especially when religious faith is repeatedly reinforced through prayer and ritual. A large body of research on religion and health has shown that religion can be beneficial for our physical, mental, and emotional health, as well as our spiritual health. In fact, various studies have found that regular participation in religious worship is associated with less hypertension, anxiety, and depression, and lower risks of coronary heart disease, stroke, cancer, chronic obstructive lung disease, disability, and mortality.[47] However, health benefits of religion may be linked more to certain health-related attributes of religion, such as discouraging high-risk behaviors, imposing dietary restrictions, and providing social support, than to religious faith *per se*.[48]

I agree with the view that religious faith operates like medical faith, albeit to a degree that is not presently known.[46,48] Then too, spiritual faith might also be at work in its own unique way.

Spiritual faith differs from religious faith, for spiritual faith originates from our spirits being connected with God rather than from our religious beliefs and practices. Spiritual faith enables us to engage in spiritual healing with firm belief and absolute trust in God, even if we ourselves have not experienced spiritual healing or have not witnessed it in others.[36,49]

No doubt, some people who come to a spiritual healing session will be concerned for not having the strength of spiritual faith that they perceive as being necessary for spiritual healing. Weak spiritual faith appears to be caused most frequently by distorted religious teachings about health conditions that lead to distorted teachings

about spiritual healing.[36] Some of the distorted religious teachings about health conditions are:
- They are necessary to help us grow spiritually, so spiritual healing is against God's will.
- They are God's punishment for personal or ancestral sin.
- They have redemptive value.

Some of the distorted religious teachings about spiritual healing are:
- It was necessary only to help get the Church started.
- It does not occur because humankind has no power over natural forces.
- It must be performed by a uniquely capable person.
- "Faith healing" (a common, erroneous term still used for spiritual healing) does not occur if one does not have enough faith to be healed.

I believe that weak spiritual faith can hamper our helping God with spiritual healing, even though our experience with spiritual healing indicates that God determines if and when it will happen. Therefore, a spiritual healing session should begin with preparations that nurture or empower our spiritual faith.

## 2. Compassion

"Compassion," along with spiritual faith, substantially participates in opening our spirits and energizing the intentionality of our praying to be channels for the healing energy of the Holy Spirit. Compassion is a combination of our becoming aware of another person's suffering and being motivated to help relieve it. Simply stated, compassion means, "I feel for you and I wish to help you."

A related word, "empathy," is our ability to imagine and experience another person's suffering. Also simply stated, empathy means, "I feel with you."

Research has found that compassion and empathy originate in different areas of our brain, which explains why empathy may not lead to the desire to be of help, or may create such emotional distress that the opposite of the desire to be of help occurs.[50] Results of studies of compassion suggest that it is both fundamental and beneficial to human survival.[51]

Jesus showed remarkable compassion throughout his ministry. He also taught its meaning in his well-known "Parable of the Lost Son" (Lk 15:11-32). This parable begins with a father dividing his estate between his two sons, one of whom leaves home and squanders it, and ends with the wayward son, out of money and starving, returning home to his father. Jesus said: "*while he* [the son] *was still far off, his father saw him and was filled with compassion; he ran and put his arms around him and kissed him*" (Lk 15:20). Jesus then described the father welcoming the "fallen" son home and providing for him.

Compassion is an expression of love for another person, in the way that our deeply compassionate God loves us.[36,52] Authentic compassion can move us into a state of caring so profound that we transcend the mental, emotional and spiritual barriers that we erect around ourselves.[45,53] When we rise above these barriers, we can pray for an ill person in a selfless, non-judgmental, and intensely loving way.

Studies are showing that mindfulness, particularly if practiced regularly, helps us to become more compassionate. Although we do not know how this positive effect of mindfulness occurs, improvement in personal relationships or interconnectedness with others observed during mindfulness training appears to be an important contributing factor. For this reason I believe that words and actions that foster mindfulness are an important part of spiritual healing sessions (see Chapter D.3.).

Finally, showing compassion breeds compassion. Therefore, we should make every effort give those who come to a session for spiritual healing of a health condition as much sincere and authentic attention as is reasonable and proper, without expressing any negative thoughts or opinions to them.[21] This attention includes offering them physical assistance and comfort, listening attentively and sympathetically to them, and touching and embracing them if and when appropriate.

## 3. Prayer

With "prayer," we humbly ask God that we may be channels for the healing energy of the Holy Spirit. We do this with an intentionality which I believe is energized by our spiritual faith and compassion.

Intentionality appears to be a quality of the human mind and spirit, in directing an intention to having a specific action.[54] It is of considerable interest to those in the scientific community who have been studying the effects of intentionality on humans and living nonhuman systems for several decades. Promoting this interest have been numerous reports of the instantaneous, spontaneous healing of various serious health conditions attributed to prayer, with much of this healing occurring at a substantial distance between the person who prays for healing and the person who receives it.[36,55,56,57] Scientists have attributed this healing at a distance to a nonlocal phenomenon which they describe in terms of quantum mechanics rather than classical physics.[58,59] This phenomenon involves an energy that transcends the usual constraints of distance through space and time, by traveling instantly and not decreasing in power by the inverse square of the distance ($1/d^2$) from its source, as do sound and light.

Numerous well-designed studies have been conducted to determine the effectiveness of intentionality as used in prayer for healing. Studies using pairs of subjects who are shielded from each other electromagnetically and acoustically have found that intentionality in one subject can generate physiological responses, including electroencephalographic (EEG) changes, in the other subject.[60] Yet studies using self-reported healers have repeatedly and unexplainably failed to show that intentionality can be effective for the distant healing of various medical conditions.[60,61,62,63]

Several large-population studies, also well designed, have attempted to determine whether intercessory prayer, or prayer for others (as opposed to petitionary prayer, or prayer for oneself), is effective in spiritual healing. Overall, they have not shown an intercessory prayer effect, making us wonder why, when we have so much anecdotal evidence to the contrary. I believe that the answer becomes apparent when we consider the design and outcomes of five major, randomized, controlled studies of intercessory prayer for spiritual healing.

- Byrd Study:[64] 393 patients who were newly admitted to a US hospital's coronary care unit (CCU) were randomized to have prayer (prayed-for group, 192 patients) or no prayer (control group, 201 patients), with neither the patients nor their caregivers being told who was to have prayer (double-blind study).

    Those who prayed were born-again Protestants and Roman Catholics. They were given the first name of each for-prayer patient, a brief description of the patient's heart problem, and told to pray daily for the patient's rapid recovery, protection from complications and death, and for anything else that they believed might be helpful to recovery. They prayed for many different patients, with each patient having five to seven persons praying for him or her while hospitalized.

    Twenty-six possible outcomes were assessed in this study. As compared to the control group of patients, 7 percent fewer patients in the prayed-for group needed antibiotics, 5 percent fewer needed diuretics, 5 percent fewer had pneumonia, 5 percent fewer had congestive heart failure, 5 percent fewer had cardiac arrest, and none required endotracheal intubation (12 patients in the control group). Byrd found that when he combined this outcomes data, the groups were separated to a highly significant degree, which led him to conclude that "intercessory prayer to the Judeo-Christian God has a beneficial therapeutic effect in patients admitted to a CCU."

- Harris Study:[65] 990 consecutive patients who were newly admitted to a US hospital's CCU were randomized to have prayer (prayed-for group, 400 patients) or no prayer (control group, 399 patients), with neither the patients nor their caregivers being told who was to have prayer (double-blind study).

Those who were to pray had to agree with statements expressing belief in God, God's concern with individual lives and God's responsiveness to prayers for healing on behalf of the sick. They were given the first name of each for-prayer patient and told to pray for the patient's recovery with no complications. Prayer was to begin the day after the patient's admission to hospital and be continued for 28 days. The persons who prayed were randomly divided into 15 groups of five persons who did not know each other. Prayer was offered individually, not in a group.

The CCU severity-adjusted, composite outcomes scores, derived from blinded, retrospective chart review, were significantly lower for the prayed-for group than the control group of patients. However, the lengths of patient stay in the CCU and hospital were not significantly different between the groups. Notably, none of the significant benefits of prayer in the Byrd study were observed in the Harris study.

- Aviles Study:[66] 799 patients who were discharged from a US hospital's CCU were randomized to have prayer (prayed-for group, 192 patients) or no prayer (control group, 201 patients), with neither the patients nor their caregivers being told who was to have prayer (double-blind study).

    Those who prayed were recruited from local religious groups and meetings with people who were interested in this study in the community. They were given the first name, age, sex, diagnosis and general condition of each for-prayer patient, and were told to pray for the patient at least once a week for 26 weeks; what they were to pray for was not stated in the report of this study. One person prayed for one to 100 (average 7.4) patients.

    At 26 weeks, the occurrence of death, cardiac arrest, coronary revascularization surgery, a re-hospitalization or emergency department visit due to cardiovascular disease was not significantly different between the prayed-for and control groups of patients, or when the prayed-for and control patients were separated into high-risk and low risk groups.

- Krucoff study:[67] 748 patients undergoing percutaneous coronary intervention or elective coronary catheterization in nine US medical centers were randomly assigned to have 40-minute sessions of bedside music, imagery, and touch (MIT) therapy or no MIT therapy; the centers were informed of these assignments. At the same time the patients were randomly assigned to have prayer or no prayer; neither the centers nor the patients were informed of these prayer assignments. Consequently, 192 patients were assigned for standard care only, 182 for prayer only, 185 for MIT therapy only, and 189 for both prayer and MIT therapy.

    In the first 2 years of this study, the name, age and medical diagnosis of each for-prayer patient were e-mailed immediately after patient randomization to each of 12 "primary-tier" established Christian, Jewish, Muslim, and Buddhist congregations. The timing and content of prayers followed the practice of each congregation, with durations ranging from 5 to 30 days after randomization. In the final year of the study, 12 "second-tier" congregations were added, but were not given any patient information. Instead, they were told to pray for those who were in the prayer group in the primary-tier.

A composite endpoint of major cardiovascular events, death, or readmission to hospital over the 6-month period following patient randomization did not differ between the two patient groups that had prayer and the two patient groups that did not have prayer. The 6-month mortality was significantly lower in the two groups that had MIT therapy than the two groups that did not have MIT therapy.

- Benson Study:[68] 1802 patients who were admitted 6 US hospitals to have coronary artery bypass graft (CABG) surgery were randomly assigned to have: prayer with the patients and their caregivers not being told so (prayed-for A group, 604 patients), to have prayer with the patients and their caregivers being told so (prayed-for B group), and to have no prayer with the patients and their caregivers not being told so (control group, 597 patients).

Those who prayed were recruited from two Roman Catholic groups and one Protestant group. They were given the first name and the first initial of the last name of each for-prayer patient, and told to pray for the patient for 14 consecutive days starting the night before scheduled surgery. These groups agreed to add the phrase, "for a successful surgery with a quick, healthy recovery and no complications" to their prayers.

The primary outcome of this study was any postoperative complication within 30 days of CABG surgery. This outcome was similar in the prayed-for the A and control groups of patients, suggesting that prayer itself had no effect on complication-free recovery from CABG surgery. Interestingly, this outcome was significantly greater in the prayed-for the B group of patients who knew they were being prayed for, than in the prayed-for the A group of patients who did not know they were being prayed for. The secondary outcome of any major event and 30-day mortality was similar in all three groups of patients.

Whereas several outcomes in Byrd study and the composite outcome scores in the Harris study suggest that prayer is effective for spiritual healing, the Byrd study outcomes were not replicated in the Harris study. Moreover, no positive outcomes occurred in the Aviles, Krucoff, or Benson studies. Why? In these and numerous other attempts to establish the effectiveness of intercessory prayer for spiritual healing, researchers have used the "scientific method," which prevents patients from knowing whether they are being prayed for or not being prayed for. Moreover, those who have done the praying have been given minimal patient information in order to assure impartiality of their prayer and to prevent non-prayer effects. In my opinion, providing the person who is to pray minimal information on a patient such as first name, the first initial of the last name, age, sex, diagnosis, and medical condition, is insufficient to establish an interpersonal relationship that is conducive to spiritual healing. Consequently, these studies have not allowed those who prayed for spiritual healing to pray for a person's healing with an intentionality energized by spiritual faith and compassion.

Whether science can establish the effectiveness of spiritual healing - specifically spiritual healing involving prayer - remains open to question. I believe that studies in which prayer given with an intentionality energized by spiritual faith and compassion will be extremely difficult, if not impossible. But are not countless anecdotal accounts of spiritual healing pointing to what the outcomes of these studies would be?

I believe that we should pray to God for spiritual healing with an attitude that enables us to communicate freely with God and in this way help God heal us. Jesus taught a right attitude, not a right formula for prayer, especially when he said, *But whenever when you pray, go into your room and shut the door and pray to your Father who is in secret* (Mt 6:6).[69] A right or spiritually healthy attitude is viewed as an acceptance rather than an expectation of God, as a giving over rather than a giving up to God, and as "being" rather than "doing" in God's presence.[56] We get ourselves into this attitude when we enter a state of mindfulness, as I describe in Chapter D.3.

We should pray to God for spiritual healing with confidence, for as Jesus said, *So I tell you, whatever you ask for in prayer believe that you have received it, and it will be yours* (Mk 11:24; see also Mt 7:7, 8 and Jn 16:23, 24).[70] Moreover, as Jesus clearly showed in his ministry, we should also pray humbly, with no thought or word being given to coercing God for a spiritual healing or even to telling God when to heal.[16,22,36]

For individual privacy under American Law, a person with a health condition must agree that any "open" prayer for the spiritual healing of the condition can include the name or a brief description of the condition. Otherwise, he or she might place a hand, if possible, over the area of her or his body that is affected or most affected by the health condition.[36,71] Prayer for spiritual healing can also be non-specific, asking God to heal with such phrases as "according to your will," "let your will be done," and "for the greater good." Every prayer for healing should acknowledge God's love for us and express our faith in God.[36]

## WE CAN HELP GOD HEAL US

A prayer for spiritual healing might include the phrase, "in the name of Jesus Christ." Jesus said, *"Very truly, I tell you, if you ask anything of the Father in my name, he will give it to you* (Jn 16:23). As I said in Chapter B.2., "in my name" in Aramaic, the language that Jesus spoke, means "as I would do it."[21] So when we add "in Jesus' name" or a similar phrase to a prayer, we taking on the personality of Jesus and praying as Jesus would have prayed.[22]

In contrast to various church liturgies for spiritual healing, I encourage spontaneous prayer for a person's spiritual healing especially during laying on of hands during a spiritual healing session. Virtually all of the spontaneous prayers that I have heard while conducting healing sessions have been appropriate and wonderful, reflecting an intentionality energized by authentic compassion for the person being prayed for.

Many people believe that prayer for spiritual healing should include a request of the angelic realm for assistance in guiding divine healing energy. Angels which serve as God's helpers figure prominently in the Holy Bible, with angelic assistance being mentioned in over half of its books and in an equal number of the books of the Old and New Testaments.[72] Their involvement with spiritual healing is reflected in the name of a prominent angel, Raphael, which in Hebrew means, "God heals."[73] The unknown author of The Letter to the Hebrews asks, *Are not all angels spirits in the divine service, sent to serve for the sake of those who are to inherit salvation* (Heb 1:14)? Spirits with a ministry have continued to intervene in history, with the majority of Christians, including renowned theologians, believing that we have at least one guardian angel or spirit guide.[27,72,73] Therefore, as I describe in my book, *Spirits Can Help God Heal Us*,[2] we might call in prayer upon the spirit world to help God in healing us.

People who attend spiritual healing sessions often describe experiencing the presence of God's Spirit. Especially while praying, they may become aware of an unseen energy felt as rush of warmth or tingling passing through the body, have momentary lightheadedness, and briefly weep. They may also hear a snapping or cracking sound like electrical static in the air. For several seconds during a spiritual healing session that I was conducting, a clear sound of shattering glass suddenly occurred for several seconds in the area of the stained glass skylight above me, with no earthly cause of this disturbance being evident.

## 4. Touch (The Laying on of Hands)

The laying on of hands for healing dates back to antiquity, as described in writings found in India, Tibet, China, Egypt, and Greece.[16,74] Jesus used the laying on of hands many times in performing spiritual healing. In the longer ending of the Gospel of Mark, he told his disciples: *"And these signs will accompany those believe: by using my name ... they will lay their hands on the sick and they will recover"* (Mk 16:17, 18). However, the book of Acts describes only one instance of spiritual healing using the laying on of hands, when Paul cured the father of Publius of a fever and dysentery (Acts 28:7, 8). Moreover, the letter of James indicates that the early Church used anointing with oil rather than the laying on of hands in its practice of spiritual healing (Jas 5:14).

In the laying on of hands we use a unique energy system throughout and surrounding each of our bodies to direct or channel the healing energy of the Holy Spirit for spiritual healing. This energy system, called the "subtle energy body," is sustained by universal vital life force energy.[75,76,77] Within us, the energy flows along a network of pathways, or meridians, and around us the energy forms an energy field, or aura.[75] The aura has seven distinct layers which are associated

## WE CAN HELP GOD HEAL US

with our physical, mental, emotional, and spiritual functions. The aura and our physical body are penetrated by seven, major, cone-shaped vortices of energy, or chakras, which are also associated with our functions, and which channel universal life force energy throughout our body The auric layers and chakras can be detected with our hands as temperature variations or tingling sensations in the hands. They can also be seen by many people in the form of various colors of the visible spectrum. Our subtle energy system is generally believed to represent the essence of our soul, or spirit.[75,77]

Imbalances in levels of energy and blockages in the flow of energy in our subtle energy system appear to cause many undesirable health conditions and be caused by many undesirable health conditions.[75] The various therapies of energy medicine, such as acupuncture, Healing Touch, and Reiki, detect and correct these imbalances and blockages, and consequently help to prevent and heal various health conditions.

To help God heal us, we should use the laying of one or both hands with prayer on the person who desires healing (direct healing) or is acting as a surrogate for another person who desires healing (distant healing). During the laying on of hands, our subtle energy body serves as a channel to receive, conduct, and transmit divine healing to the person for whom are praying.

I recommend that the leader of a spiritual healing session invite everyone who attends a healing service to participate in the laying on of hands in order to maximize the flow of divine healing energy to the person being prayed for. However, those who do not wish to participate in a laying on of hands should be asked to sit or stand quietly aside in quiet prayer or meditation for the healing of those who are receiving the laying on of hands.

The persons who participate in a laying on of hands should stand or kneel around the individual who desires spiritual healing and is seated comfortably in a chair that can be surrounded those who will be engaged in the laying on of hands with prayer. Each participant in the laying on of hands should gently place one or both of their hands on the individual who desires spiritual healing, or on another person in line of contact with that individual. All hands should remain in position as the participants initially pray together and, if they wish, individually for the person's healing, over a period of up to several minutes. Finally, the session leader should close the laying on of hands with a prayer of gratitude to God for the healing presence of the Holy Spirit.

An individual who receives the laying on of hands may need assistance with rising and taking a few steps, due to weakness and unsteadiness, attributed to markedly increased exposure to universal vital life force energy. Also, people who receive the laying on of hands and many who participate in the laying on of hands with prayer weep, so tissue should be available to everyone.

Finally, ample time must be allowed for the laying on of hands with prayer for each person who may request spiritual healing. To prevent a spiritual healing session from becoming uncomfortably long, I recommend that when many attend a spiritual healing session, more than one group for this should be set up, each with a leader, ready for the laying on of hands with prayer.

## 5. Repeat Healing Sessions

Spiritual healing is a process, so that a single spiritual healing session may be insufficient to heal a health condition, especially if it is chronic or severe. Therefore, one or more repeat spiritual healing sessions may be necessary to complete and sustain the healing of a health condition.[35,36] Moreover, the duration of one or more repeat spiritual healing sessions for certain persons might have to be increased to one or more hours, as so-called "soaking prayer."

## D. PREPARATION FOR A SPIRITUAL HEALING SESSION

Jesus' ways of spiritual healing clearly show how we can help God heal us. But before we give this help, I believe that appropriate preparations should be made for doing so. First, the setting for a spiritual healing session should be made as "spiritual" as possible for everyone who will be involved in it. Second, a session should be described and any questions on its purpose and conduct should be answered before it begins. Third, mindfulness while engaged in spiritual healing should be generated or enhanced. Fourth, anyone who wishes to have distant spiritual healing should give advance permission for it, and agree be in an uninterrupted state of prayer during the spiritual healing session in which they will receive distant spiritual healing.

Spiritual healing should be conducted in an environment that is quiet, comfortable and welcoming. The participants in a spiritual healing session should be protected from distracting sights and sounds. Bright lights should be lowered and possibly softened by candle light, and extraneous noise should be masked by soft and "inspiring" background music. Before a session begins, its leader should warmly greet all participants, and encourage them to introduce themselves to each other in the spirit of love.

Every person who attends a spiritual healing session should be provided a booklet containing the purpose and outline of the session, directions to follow throughout the session, and prayers to be used during the session. Additions to the booklet might be biblical and nonbiblical stories and pictures of spiritual healing down through the ages, testimonials that support of reality of spiritual healing, references to major books and articles on spiritual healing, the sources of music being played during the healing service, and the names and brief résumés of gifted healers throughout history.

A person who desires direct or distant (as a surrogate) spiritual healing of a health condition should be seated in an open space, in an armchair that gives both comfort and support. This arrangement should allow all who wish to help God heal a comfortable place to sit or stand for up to several minutes while engaged in touch and prayer for healing. As mentioned above, spontaneous weeping is common during spiritual healing sessions, so boxes of tissue should be readily available.

## 2. Understanding

For those who wish to help God heal us by participating in a spiritual healing session, but are unsure of what spiritual healing involves, I recommend that a session leader give a brief, informative talk about spiritual healing before every spiritual healing session begins. This talk about spiritual healing might include:

- God creates a universal vital life force energy with the power to heal us. We can use this energy in various spiritually empowered ways, as shown to us by Jesus Christ, to channel this energy to help God heal us.
- As I describe in Chapter C., spiritual faith, along with compassion, substantially participates in opening our spirits and energizing the intentionality of our praying for us to be channels for the healing energy of the God's Spirit. One might say that everything said and done during a spiritual healing session should reflect the intentionality of the session and each participant in it - the spiritual healing of a person or persons who are suffering from a health condition.
- The words, spiritual healing, can mean God's use of universal vital life force energy to heal us or our channeling this energy to help God heal us. They can mean the process of healing by

## WE CAN HELP GOD HEAL US

universal life force energy. Finally, they can mean improving or curing a health condition by God, with or without our help.
- Spiritual healing can be either improvement or cure of a health condition using the healing energy of God's Spirit. When we help God with spiritual healing we lay our hands on a person suffering from a health condition and ask God in prayer to enable us to receive, conduct, and transmit this divine energy to heal the health condition. Everyone has the ability to channel the energy, either as a special or as a natural gift from God.
- Improvement of a health condition by spiritual healing is most often transformational in nature, such as maintaining strength and balance in body, mind, and spirit while suffering from a health condition, adjusting to physical or mental limitations being produced by a health condition, and accepting the love of God, family, and friends when approaching death from a health condition. Cure of a health condition by spiritual healing is complete healing of the condition, although some disability from a cured health condition may remain.
- Direct spiritual healing is performed on a person who is with us to receive the healing, and distant spiritual healing is performed on a person who is not with us to receive the healing. Although distant spiritual healing is usually performed with prayer, it can also be performed in the same way as a direct spiritual healing by using a stand-in person, or surrogate, to represent the person who is not present to receive direct spiritual healing.
- Experience with spiritual healing has shown that God determines if and when a spiritual healing will happen.

- Spiritual healing may occur immediately or gradually. One or more spiritual healing sessions, or a longer session, may be necessary for healing to happen or persist.
- The Holy Bible describes spiritual healing, particularly by Jesus, his disciples, and his Apostles. Also, spiritual healing has continued to occur since biblical times.
- Jesus showed us ways to help God heal us that involves spiritual faith, compassion, prayer, and, for direct and distant (with a surrogate) healing, touch as the laying on of hands. Jesus' ways of spiritual healing will be used in this spiritual healing session.
- Many people believe or are inclined to believe that their health condition is God's punishment for sin. Jesus never asked anyone who came to him for spiritual healing what sin he or she, or even an ancestor had committed that deserved God's punishment their health condition. In fact, Jesus told his disciples that he did not believe God punishes sin with a health condition.
- Spiritual healing is not a replacement for medical care, but we are always welcome to help God heal us.

## 3. Mindfulness

All who are to participate in spiritual healing session, including those who wish to receive spiritual healing, should be given the opportunity to enter -a state of mindfulness for what they will be doing: actually helping God with healing. Mindfulness is our innate ability to be fully in the present moment, aware of who we are and what we are doing. It allows us to embrace what is happening, without resistance or fear.[78]

Maintaining mindfulness involves keeping our minds centered, free of thoughts that dwell on the past or envision the future. It also involves returning our minds to the present when they drift away, as we do in various forms of meditation.

Active attention on the present – being mindful – enables us to focus our attention on the need for others' well-being.[79] Most especially, it enables us to develop compassion with our desire and capacity to help God with their healing, as I described in Chapter C.2.

Among the various means that I use to intensify mindfulness in a spiritual healing session are, in order: words of inspiration, words of welcome, a reading or readings from scripture, a song or songs, a short message, a guided meditation, The Lord's Prayer, and a general prayer for healing. An example of each follows.

### Words of Inspiration
Good people,
Most royal greening verdancy,
Rooted in the sun,
You shine with radiant light.
In this circle of earthly existence
You shine so finely,
It surpasses understanding.
God hugs you.
You are encircled by the arms of the mystery of God.

Hildegard of Bingen[80]

### Words of Welcome
Welcome to everyone who has come to our spiritual healing session. First we will fully open our minds and spirits to God. Then those who desire spiritual healing of themselves or persons who are not here will be invited to come forward, so that we may lay our hands upon them and pray for their healing. The laying on of hands is an ancient, universal, religious practice for channeling the healing energy of the Holy Spirit to those who desire healing of themselves or others.

I now invite you to welcome those around you in the spirit of love.

## A Reading from Scripture

Jesus of Nazareth was a remarkable in helping God with spiritual healing. Moreover, and he commissioned his disciples to go out into the world to do so, as well as to teach and preach, as he did. Spiritual healing has continued in the Church to this day. In the following readings from the Gospels of Matthew and John, Jesus heals people who are able and unable to come to him, as we will ask and help God to do in this spiritual healing session.

*When Jesus had come down from the mountain, great crowds followed him; and there was a leper who came to him and knelt before him, saying, "Lord, if you choose, you can make me clean." He reached out his hand and touched him, saying, "I do choose. Be made clean!"' Immediately his leprosy was cleansed* (Mt 8:1-3)

*Then he [Jesus] came again to Cana in Galilee where he had changed the water into wine. Now there was a royal official whose son lay ill in Capernaum. When he heard that Jesus had come from Judea to Galilee, he went and begged him to come down and heal his son, for he was at the point of death. Then Jesus said to him, "Unless you see signs and wonders you will not believe." The official said to him, "Sir, come down before my little boy dies." Jesus said to him, "Go; your son will live." The man believed the word that Jesus spoke to him and started on his way. As he was going down, his slaves* met *him and told him that his child was alive. So he asked them the hour when he began to recover, and they said to him, "Yesterday at one in the afternoon the fever left him" The father realized that this was hour when Jesus had said to him, "Your son will live." So he himself believed, along with his whole household"* (Jn 4:46-53).

# WE CAN HELP GOD HEAL US

**A Song**
Spirit of the Living God, fall afresh on me.[81]
Spirit of the living God, fall afresh on me.
Melt me, mold me, fill me, use me.
Spirit of the living God, fall afresh on me.

**A Short Message**
In the Gospel of Mark, Jesus said, *"Truly I tell you, if you say to this mountain, 'Be taken up and thrown into the sea', and if you do not doubt in your heart, but believe that what you say will come to pass, it will be done for you. So I tell you, whatever you ask for in prayer, believe that you have received it, and it will be yours."* (Mk 11:23-24).

In this gospel passage, Jesus is reassuring his disciples about the power of prayer as he gives them the knowledge and experience necessary to carry on his ministry, including spiritual healing, when he is no longer with them. We might wonder: Why did Jesus have to give the disciples this reassurance when, according to the Gospels, he had already empowered them for spiritual healing and sent them out to heal with remarkable success? An appropriate answer to this question might be that Jesus' disciples, being ordinary people like us, were prone to need reassurance of God's love and support while being trained to carry on Jesus' very challenging ministry.

Do we also need to be reassured that spiritual healing still occurs? If so, we can look back at the long history of spiritual healing and even listen to persons who have experienced it. Whether or not we need this reassurance, Jesus is telling us that when we really believe that prayer for healing works, it will!

Soon we will use the laying on of hands with prayer to channel the healing energy of God's Spirit to help God heal those with health conditions who are here and not here with us and desire to receive spiritual healing of their conditions. Although the prayer we will use during the laying on of hands asks for healing "according to God's will," the person for whom we are praying may also wish that we pray for the healing of a specific health condition.

Spiritual healing can be either improvement or cure of a health condition. Improvement of a health condition by spiritual healing is most often transformational in nature, such as maintaining strength and balance in body, mind, and spirit while suffering from the condition, adjusting to physical or mental limitations being produced by the condition, and accepting the love of God, family, and friends when approaching death from the condition. Cure of a health condition by spiritual healing is complete healing of the condition, although some disability from the condition may remain.

We may believe that God can punish us for a sin with a health condition. However, Jesus would tell us that God does do this, but out of unconditional love for us wants us to be well in body, mind, and spirit.

## A Guided Meditation

The following guided meditation help us get into a spiritually healthy attitude for helping God with spiritual healing, by calming our minds and clearing them of troublesome thoughts and emotions.

Let us prepare ourselves for the meditation by relaxing comfortably in our chairs, with our hands apart on our laps and our feet flat on the floor. Now close your eyes, and breathe slowly and deeply three times, in through your nose and out through your mouth. *(Accompany this exercise with, "in through your nose and out through your mouth.")*

# WE CAN HELP GOD HEAL US

Imagine that you are alone on a beach on a warm summer day, walking barefoot on a stretch of sand kept moist by small waves washing onto the shore. To your right the dark blue water stretches to the horizon, where it blends with the cloudless blue sky. *(Pause)* To your left are small dunes of fine, rippled sand capped by tall grass, swaying in the gentle breeze. *(Pause)*

You stop and look at the water, sky and sand, and momentarily experience being at peace. *(Pause)* You ask yourself, "Why can't I feel this way all the time? *(Pause)* Almost immediately an inner voice replies: "Because your mind is cluttered with so many troublesome thoughts and emotions." *(Pause)* Then the voice tells you, "Go to the water's edge and write a thought or emotion that is bothering you in the moist sand, and let a wave come and wash it away." *(Pause)*

You pick up a small, smooth stick, and kneel at the water's edge. As a wave recedes you write in the sand, "fear," which is washed away by the next wave. *(Pause)* Then you write "guilt," which is washed away by the next wave. *(Pause)* (*Repeat separately for anger, resentment, remorse, jealousy, doubt, despair, sorrow, etc.) (Pause)*

When you have nothing more to write in the sand and be washed away, you realize that you are again experiencing being at peace, and that this time it does not go away. You continue walking along the beach, enjoying its beauty. *(Pause)*

You may open your eyes when you wish.

**The Lord's Prayer**

Our Father, who art in heaven, hallowed be thy name. Thy kingdom come. Thy will be done on earth as it is in heaven. Give us this day our daily bread. And forgive us our trespasses, as we forgive those who trespass against us. And do not lead us into temptation, but deliver us from evil. For thine is the kingdom, and the power, and the glory, for ever. Amen.

**A General Prayer for Healing**
 All-powerful and loving God, we welcome you among us at this session for spiritual healing. With open minds and spirits, we wish to help you in healing those of us with various health conditions, as did Jesus Christ. Amen.

## 4. Permission

All who wish to have a have spiritual healing, whether direct healing, distant healing through a surrogate, or simply distant healing, must give permission for it in advance of spiritual healing being performed on them. As required in the United States under the Health Insurance Portability and Accountability Act of 1996, they must also give permission for their names and health conditions to be revealed or otherwise mentioned in a spiritual healing session. For those who do not wish to disclose their health condition, God should be asked for their spiritual healing using such phrases as "according to your will," "let your will be done," and "for your greatest good."

# E. A SPIRITUAL HEALING SESSION

## 1. Framework

*(Background Music)*

**Words of Inspiration** *(Leader or Reader) (see **E.2. Resources**)*

**Welcome** *(Leader)*

Welcome to everyone who has come to our spiritual healing session. First we will fully open our minds and spirits to God. Then those who desire spiritual healing of themselves or persons who are not here will be invited to come forward individually, so that we may lay our hands upon them and pray for healing. The laying on of hands is an ancient, universal, religious practice for channeling the healing energy of the Holy Spirit to those who desire healing of themselves or others.

I now invite you to welcome those around you in the spirit of love.

**Scripture** *(Leader or Reader) (see **E.2. Resources**)*
*New Testament passages might be preceded by:*

Jesus of Nazareth was a remarkable spiritual healer, and he commissioned his disciples to go out into the world to heal, as well as to teach and preach, as he did. Spiritual healing has continued in the Church to this day. In the following readings from the Gospels of _____ and _____, Jesus helps God to heal people who were able and unable to come to Jesus, as we will ask and help God to heal in this spiritual healing session.

**Song** (All) *(see **E.2. Resources**)*

**Message** *(Leader) (see **E.2. Resources**)*
*The message might be ended with:*
Soon we will use the laying on of hands with prayer to channel the healing energy of God's Spirit to help God heal those with health conditions who are here and not here with us, and desire to receive spiritual healing of their health conditions. Although the prayer that we will use during the laying on of hands asks for healing "according to God's will," a person for whom we will be praying may wish that we pray for the healing of a specific health condition.

Spiritual healing can be either improvement or cure of a health condition. Improvement of a health condition by spiritual healing is most often transformational in nature, such as maintaining strength and balance in body, mind, and spirit while suffering from a health condition, adjusting to physical or mental limitations being produced by a health condition, and accepting the love of God, family, and friends when approaching death from a health condition. Cure of a health condition by spiritual healing is complete healing of the condition, although some disability from the condition may remain.

We may believe that God can punish us for a sin with a health condition. However, Jesus would tell us that God does not do this, but out of unconditional love wants us to be well in body, mind, and spirit.

**Guided Meditation** *(Leader or Reader) (see **E.2. Resources**)*
*A guided meditation might be preceded by:*
The following guided meditation help us get into a spiritually healthy attitude for helping God with spiritual healing, by calming our minds and clearing them of troublesome thoughts and emotions.

**Solo or Song** (All) *(see **E.2. Resources**)*

**A General Prayer for Healing** (All) *(see **E.2. Resources**)*

# WE CAN HELP GOD HEAL US

**The Lord's Prayer** (All) *("Trespasses ... trespass" or "sins ... sin" are preferred. "And do not lead us into temptation might be changed to "And do not leave us in temptation.")*

**The Laying on of Hands**

You are now invited to participate the laying on of hands with prayer. Those who do not wish to participate in the laying on of hands are asked remain in prayer or meditation for healing.

*With hands being laid upon a person who desires his or her own healing -*

(All) _____, **we lay our hands upon you to help you receive the healing energy of God's Spirit. With faith in God** *(may add "and in the name of Jesus Christ")*, **we pray for your healing according to God's will.**

(Leader): You are invited to give additional prayers for _____'s healing.

*With hands being laid upon a person who desires another person's healing -*

**(All)** _____, **we lay our hands upon you to help you receive and send the healing energy of God's Spirit to** _____. **With faith in God** *(may add "and in the name of Jesus Christ")*, **we pray for his/her healing according to God's will.**

(Leader): You are invited to give additional prayers for _____'s healing.

**A Prayer of Thankfulness** (All) *(see E.2. Resources)*

**Song** (All) *(see E.2. Resources)*

**A Blessing** *(Leader) (see **E.2. Resources**)*

## 2. Resources

### Words of Inspiration
*The Lord is my shepherd, I shall not want.*
  *He makes me lie down in green pastures;*
*he leads me beside still waters;*
  *he restores my soul.*
*He leads me in right paths*
  *for his name's sake.*

*Even though I walk through the darkest valley,*
  *I fear no evil;*
*for you are with me;*
  *your rod and your staff—*
  *they comfort me.*

*Surely goodness and mercy shall follow me*
  *all the days of my life,*
*and I shall dwell in the house of the Lord*
  *my whole life long.*

Psalm 23:1-4, 6

*I cry aloud to God,*
  *aloud to God, that he may hear me.*
*In the day of my trouble I seek the Lord;*
  *in the night my hand is stretched out without wearying;*
  *my soul refuses to be comforted.*
*And I say, "It is my grief*
  *that the right hand of the Most High has changed."*

*I will call to mind the deeds of the L*ORD*;*
  *I will remember your wonders of old.*
*I will meditate on all your work,*
  *and muse on your mighty deeds.*

Psalm 77:1, 2, 11-12

# WE CAN HELP GOD HEAL US

*I lift up my eyes to the hills—*
  *from where will my help come?*
*My help comes from the LORD,*
  *who made heaven and earth.*

*He will not let your foot be moved;*
  *he who keeps you will not slumber.*
*The LORD is your keeper;*
  *the LORD is your shade at your right hand.*
*The sun shall not strike you by day,*
  *nor the moon by night.*

*The LORD will keep you from all evil;*
  *he will keep your life.*
*The Lord will keep*
  *your going out and your coming in*
  *from this time on and fo evermore.*

Psalm 121:1-3, 5-8

*Have you not known? Have you not heard?*
*The LORD is the everlasting God,*
  *the Creator of the ends of the earth.*
*He does not faint or grow weary;*
  *his understanding is unsearchable.*
*He gives power to the faint,*
  *and strengthens the powerless.*
*Even youths will faint and be weary,*
  *and the young will fall exhausted;*
*but those who wait for the Lord shall renew their strength,*
  *they shall mount up with wings like eagles,*
*they shall run and not be weary,*
  *they shall walk and not faint.*

Isaiah 40:28-31

## DOUGLAS E. BUSBY

*Sing for joy, O heavens, and exult, O earth;*
  *break forth, O mountains, into singing!*
*For the LORD has comforted his people,*
  *and will have compassion on his suffering ones.*

Isaiah 49:13

Jesus said, "*Ask, and it will be given to you; search, and you will find; knock, and the door will be opened for you. For everyone who asks receives, and everyone who searches finds, and for everyone who knocks, the door will be opened.*"

Matthew 7:7, 8

Jesus answered them, "Have faith in God. *Truly I tell you, if you say to this mountain, 'Be taken up and thrown into the sea', and if you do not doubt in your heart, but believe that what you say will come to pass, it will be done for you. So I tell you, whatever you ask for in prayer, believe that you have received it, and it will be yours.*"

Mark 11:22-24

The apostle Paul wrote, *Blessed be the God and Father of our Lord Jesus Christ, the Father of mercies and the God of all consolation, who consoles us in all our affliction, so that we may be able to console those who are in any affliction with the consolation with which we ourselves are consoled by God.*

2 Corinthians 1:3, 4

The apostle Paul wrote, *Do not worry about anything, but in everything by prayer and supplication with thanksgiving let your requests be made known to God. And the peace of God, which surpasses all understanding, will guard your hearts and your minds in Christ Jesus.*

Philippians 4:6, 7

# WE CAN HELP GOD HEAL US

Good people,
Most royal greening verdancy,
Rooted in the sun,
You shine with radiant light.
In this circle of earthly existence
You shine so finely,
It surpasses understanding.
God hugs you.
You are encircled by the arms of the mystery of God.

                                                Hildegard of Bingen[80]

Let nothing disturb you,
   let nothing dismay you.
All things pass
God never changes.
Patience attains all that it strives for.
Those who have God
   find they lack for nothing.
God alone suffices.

                                                 Teresa of Avila[82]

O Hidden Life, vibrant in every atom,
O Hidden Light, shining in every creature,
O Hidden Love, embracing all in Oneness,
May we who feel ourselves as one with You
Know we are therefore one with every other.

                                        Annie Besant[83] (adapted)

You carry the cure within you.
Everything that comes your way is blessed.
The Creator gives you one more day.
Stand on the neck of Fearful Mind.
Do not wait to open your heart.
Let yourself go into the Mystery.

## DOUGLAS E. BUSBY

Sometimes the threads have no weave.
The price of not loving yourself is high.

              Jim Cohn[84]

You could make this place alive,
 divine, infused with inner light.
You can take your shy, secret hopes
 and construct them into what they might.
The place can be anywhere.
The only source is within you.
All that you see was once a dream.
Dream again today and that you do become.

              Barry Harris[85]

May we learn to open in love
so all the doors and windows
of our bodies swing wide
on their rusty hinges.

May we learn to give ourselves with both hands,
to lift each other on our shoulders,
to carry one another along.

May holiness move in us
so we may pay attention to its small voice
and honor its light in each other.

             Dawna Markova[86]

Your name is our healing, O our God, and remembrance of You is our remedy. Nearness to You is our hope, and love for You is our compassion. Your mercy to us is our healing and our succor in both this world and the world to come. You, truly, are the All-Bountiful, the All-Knowing, the All-Wise.

            Baha'u'llah[87] (adapted)

# WE CAN HELP GOD HEAL US

God's love shines brightly,
  fully revealing,
  wholly embracing,
  while we pray for healing.

God's love shines brightly,
  given graciously,
  received thankfully,
  whiles we pray for healing.

Douglas Busby

## Scripture

<u>Example of direct spiritual healing in the Old Testament - Elijah helps God to revive the widow's son</u>

*After this the son of the woman, the mistress of the house, became ill; his illness was so severe that there was no breath left in him. She then said to Elijah, "What have you against me, O man of God? You have come to me to bring my sin to remembrance, and to cause the death of my son!" But he said to her, "Give me your son." He took him from her bosom, carried him up into the upper chamber where he was lodging, and laid him on his own bed. He cried out to the LORD, "O LORD my God, have you brought calamity even upon the widow with whom I am staying, by killing her son?" Then he stretched himself upon the child three times, and cried out to the LORD, "O LORD my God, let this child's life come into him again." The LORD listened to the voice of Elijah; the life of the child came into him again, and he revived.*

1 Kings 17:17-22

<u>Another example of direct spiritual healing in the New Testament - Elisha helps God to cure Naaman, the commander of a foreign army, of leprosy</u>

*So Naaman came with his horses and chariots, and halted at the entrance of Elisha's house. Elisha sent a messenger to him, saying, "Go, wash in the Jordan seven times, and your flesh shall be restored* and you shall be clean." *But Naaman became angry and went away, saying, "I thought that for me he would surely come out, and stand and call on the name of the* LORD *his God, and would wave his hand over the spot, and cure the leprosy! Are not Abana and Pharpar, the rivers of Damascus, better than all the waters of Israel? Could I not wash in them, and be clean?" He turned and went away in a rage. But his servants approached and said to him, "Father, if the prophet had commanded you to do something difficult, would you not have done it? How much more, when all he said to you was, 'Wash, and be clean.'" So he went down and immersed himself seven times in the Jordan, according to the word of the man of God; his flesh was restored like the flesh of a young boy, and he was clean.*

2 Kings 5:9-14

Example of direct spiritual healing in the Gospels - Jesus helps God to heal a man with leprosy

*When Jesus had come down from the mountain, great crowds followed him; and there was a leper who came to him and knelt before him, saying, "Lord, if you choose, you can make me clean." He stretched out his hand and touched him, saying, "I do choose. Be made clean!" Immediately his leprosy was cleansed.*

Matthew 8:1-3

Other examples of direct spiritual healing in the Gospels
See Mark 7:32-35 (healing of a deaf and mute man); Luke 13:10-14 (healing of a crippled woman); John 9:1-7 (healing of a man born blind)

Example of distant spiritual healing in the Gospels - Jesus helps God to heal the royal official's son

*Then he [Jesus] came again to Cana in Galilee where he had changed the water into wine. Now there was a royal official whose son lay ill in Capernaum. When he heard that Jesus had come from Judea to Galilee, he went and begged him to come down and heal his son, for*

# WE CAN HELP GOD HEAL US

*he was at the point of death. Then Jesus said to him, "Unless you see signs and wonders you will not believe." The official said to him, "Sir, come down before my little boy dies." Jesus said to him, "Go; your son will live." The man believed the word that Jesus spoke to him and started on his way. As he was going down, his slaves met him and told him that his child was alive. So he asked them the hour when he began to recover, and they said to him, "Yesterday at one in the afternoon the fever left him." The father realized that this was the hour when Jesus had said to him, "Your son will live." So he himself believed, along with his whole household.*

John 4:46-53

A similar example of distant spiritual healing in the Gospels
See Matthew 8:5-13 (healing of the Centurion's servant)

Example of direct spiritual healing in Acts - Peter helps God to heal the paralytic at Lydda
*Now as Peter went here and there among all the believers, he came down also to the saints living in Lydda. There he found a man named Aeneas, who had been bedridden for eight years, for he was paralyzed. Peter said to him, "Aeneas, Jesus Christ heals you; get up and make your bed!" And immediately he got up.*

Acts 9:32-34

Another example of direct spiritual healing in Acts - Paul helps God to heal the father of the chief official of the island of Malta
*Now in the neighborhood of that place were lands belonging to the leading man of the island, named Publius, who received us and entertained us hospitably for three days. It so happened that the father of Publius lay sick in bed with fever and dysentery. Paul visited him and cured him by praying and putting his hands on him.*

Acts 28:7, 8

## DOUGLAS E. BUSBY

**Songs**

All people that on earth do dwell,[88]
sing out your faith with cheerful voice;
Delight in God whose praise you tell,
whose presence calls you to rejoice.

Know that there is one God indeed,
who fashions us without our aid,
Who claims us, gives us all we need,
whose tender care will never fade.

Precious Lord, take my hand,[89]
lead me on, let me stand,
I am tired, I am weak, I am worn;
Through the storm, through the night,
lead me on to the light:
Take my hand, precious Lord, lead me home.

--------

Spirit of the Living God, fall afresh on me.[81]
Spirit of the living God, fall afresh on me.
Melt me, mold me, fill me, use me.
Spirit of the living God, fall afresh on me.

--------

Breathe on me, Breath of God,[90]
fill me with life anew,
that I may love the way you love,
and do what you would do.

Breathe on me, Breath of God,
stir in me one desire:
That every earthly part of me
may glow with earthly fire.

--------

Amazing grace, how sweet the sound[91]

## WE CAN HELP GOD HEAL US

that saved a soul like me!
I once was lost, but now am found,
was blind but now I see.
My God has promised good to me,
whose word my hope secures;
God will my shield and portion be
as long as life endures.


This little light of mine,[92]
I'm gonna let it shine.
This little light of mine,
I'm gonna let it shine.
This little light of mine,
I'm gonna let it shine,
Let it shine, let it shine, let it shine.

--------

O Holy Spirit, Root of life,[93]
Creator, cleanser of all things,
anoint our wounds, awaken us
with lustrous movement of your wings.

O Holy Wisdom, Soaring Power,
encompass us with wings unfurled
and carry us, encircling all,
above, below, and through the world.

--------

For the beauty of the earth,[94]
for the splendor of the skies,
for the love which from our birth,
over and around us lies,
*God of all, to you we raise*

*this our song of grateful praise.*

For the joy of human love,
brother, sister, parent, child,
friends on earth, and friends above,
for all gentle thoughts and mild ,
*God of all, ...*



Open my eyes, that I may see[95]
glimpses of truth thou hast for me;
place in my hands the wonderful key
that shall unclasp and set me free.
*Silently now I wait for thee*
*ready, my God, thy will to see.*
*Open my eyes, illumine me,*
*Spirit divine!*

Open my ears, that I may hear
voices of truth thou sendest clear;
and while the wave-notes fall on my ear,
everything false will disappear.
*Silently now ...*

Open my mouth, and let me bear
gladly the warm truth everywhere;
open my heart and let me prepare
love with thy children thus to share.
*Silently now ...*

-------

Come forth , O Love divine,[96]
seek now this soul of mine,
and visit it with your own ardor glowing;

# WE CAN HELP GOD HEAL US

O Comforter, draw near,
within my heart appear,
and kindle it, your holy flame bestowing.

And so the yearning strong
with which the soul; will long,
shall far out-pass the power of human telling;
For none can guess its grace,
till love create a place
wherein the Holy Spirit makes a dwelling.

## Messages

Example 1

Jesus said, *"Ask, and it will be given to you; search, and you will find; knock, and the door will be opened for you. For everyone who asks receives, and everyone who searches finds, and for everyone who knocks, the door will be opened"* (Mt 7:7, 8).

When we knock on a door to ask the person who opens it for something, we must be prepared to speak openly and clearly. Likewise, when we knock on the door to the heavenly realm to ask God for spiritual healing, we must be prepared to pray openly and clearly. This preparation involves focusing our minds and spirits on connecting with God in prayer, or as Jesus said, getting into the right attitude for prayer. This is what we are doing as we prepare to pray for the spiritual healing of those who are with us and not with us.

Do we need to be reassured that spiritual healing still occurs? If so, we can look back at the historical reality of spiritual healing and even listen to persons who have experienced it. Whether or not we need this reassurance, Jesus is telling us that when we really believe that prayer for spiritual healing works, it will!

*(See additional paragraphs under **E.1. Framework; Message**.)*

### Example 2

Jesus said, *"Truly I tell you, if you say to this mountain, 'Be taken up and thrown into the sea', and if you do not doubt in your heart, but believe that what you say will come to pass, it will be done for you. So I tell you, whatever you ask for in prayer, believe that you have received it, and it will be yours"* (Mk 11:23, 24).

In this passage from the Gospel of Mark, Jesus is reassuring his disciples about the power of prayer, as he gives them the knowledge and experience necessary to carry on his ministry, including spiritual healing, when he is no longer with them. We might wonder: Why did Jesus have to give the disciples this reassurance when, according to the Gospels, he had already empowered them for spiritual healing and sent them out to heal with remarkable success? An appropriate answer to this question might be that Jesus' disciples, being ordinary people like us, were prone to need reassurance of God's love and support while being trained for such an intensely challenging ministry.

Do we need to be reassured that spiritual healing still occurs? If so, we can look back at the long history of spiritual healing and even listen to persons who have experienced it. Whether or not we need this reassurance, Jesus is telling us that when we really believe that prayer for healing works, it will!

*(See additional paragraphs under **E.1. Framework; Message**.)*

### Example 3

A traditional Hebrew prayer[97] suggests that angels can be all around us:

> In the Name of God the Almighty,
> To my right Michael, and to my left Gabriel,
> And before me Uriel, and behind me Raphael,
> And over my head, the presence of God.

Human beings have always had an interest in certain spiritual beings, to whom God has given special responsibilities in heaven and on earth. We call them "angels," which comes from the ancient Hebrew word for "messengers from God." The names of some of these angels, such as Michael, Gabriel, Uriel, and Raphael, are quite familiar to Jews, Christians, and Muslims alike. Interestingly, the name, Raphael, translates from Hebrew to English as, "God heals."

Throughout the ages, numerous people have described so-called "guardian angels" or "spirit guides," which protect them from sudden physical danger, even death. And many people - particularly those involved in spiritual healing – are convinced that the spirit world can help God heal us by knowing what health condition we are suffering from, and then "guiding" God's healing energy to help correct it.

Whether or not we believe that heavenly beings can help God in healing our physical, mental, emotional or spiritual health conditions, we know that only God makes spiritual healing possible for us. And even though we may pray to God, or both to God and the spirit world for healing, we must in faith "let go and let God" help us with our healing.

*(See additional paragraphs under **E.1. Framework; Message**.)*

Example 4

Dom Hélder Câmera, a great Roman Catholic archbishop who had deep concern for the poor of Brazil, wrote a poem about his life:[80]

> When I was a youngster
> > I wanted to go out running
> > among the mountain peaks.
> And when, between two summits
> > a gap appeared,
> > why not leap across the chasm?
> Led by the angel's hand,
> > all my life long
> > this is what happened,
> > this, exactly.

This wonderful poem reminds us that when we were youngsters, we believed that we could overcome life's problems if we really set our minds to it. But as adults we soon learned that usually we can resolve these problems, and that sometimes we need help with resolving them.

A serious physical, mental, emotional or spiritual health condition can prevent us from living a creative and joyful life. Yet, as the archbishop's poem says, a divine hand is always available to help us resolve whatever problem faces us. And so we reach out to God in prayer, asking that we may work hand-in-hand with God in our spiritual healing.

*(See additional paragraphs under **E.1. Framework; Message**.)*

Example 5

Amelia Earhart, the great female aviator of the 1930's, wrote a poem about courage:[83]

> Courage is the price that life exacts
>    for granting peace.
> The soul that knows it not,
>    knows no release
>    from the little things;
> Knows not the livid loneliness of fear,
>    nor mountain heights
>    where bitter joy can hear
>    the sound of wings.

Amelia Earhart was a great pioneer in aviation who faced many life-threatening challenges in flying airplanes great record-breaking distances. In 1937, her last and greatest challenge - flying around the world - ended tragically somewhere in the South Pacific.

In this wonderful poem, Amelia is giving us a clear message. She is saying that we need to have courage in order to overcome life's challenges, most especially the "livid loneliness of fear." How well her

## WE CAN HELP GOD HEAL US

words echo what we experience when challenged by a serious health condition. We certainly can be fearful and lack courage! But we can overcome our fear and generate courage with the certain knowledge that God wishes us to be whole physically, mentally, emotionally and spiritually, and can help us heal.
*(See additional paragraphs under **E.1. Framework; Message**.)*

## Guided Meditations
Example 1

Let us prepare ourselves for this meditation by relaxing comfortably in our chairs, with our hands apart on our laps and our feet flat on the floor. Now close your eyes and breathe slowly and deeply three times, in through your nose and out through your mouth. *(Accompany the breathing exercise with "in through your nose and out through your mouth.")*

Imagine that you are driving your car out in the country on a warm summer afternoon, to enjoy a few moments of peace in this hustle-bustle world. Lost in thought you turn onto a road that takes you into a dense forest that is unfamiliar to you. *(Pause)* As you slow the car, wondering where you are, you notice a narrow, winding path going into the forest, with a small sign posted next to the start of the path. You stop and back up the car to read the sign, which in golden letters announces, "Sanctuary, Welcome!" Curious as to what this sign means and where the path goes, you park the car by the side of the road, get out of it, and begin to walk on the path into the forest. *(Pause)*

You find the cool, fresh air of the forest soothing. You smell many delightful fragrances coming from the bed of brightly-colored flowers bordering the path as it winds through the forest. You stop to look upwards, and see that the trees frame a rich blue sky, making its few puffy clouds seem even whiter. You hear birds singing to each other all around you. "What a wonderful place" you say to yourself, as you become even more inquisitive and decide to continue walking. *(Pause)*

After several minutes you come upon a small meadow of ankle-deep grass, swaying gently back and forth. You walk out of the forest into the meadow to enjoy the simple beauty of the grass below you, the trees around you and the sky above you. *(Pause).* You realize that

# WE CAN HELP GOD HEAL US

you could be enjoying this moment even more if your mind could be clear of concerns and emotions that are bothering you.

While standing in the meadow, you feel a warm wind on your face, as though a gentle hand is caressing it. You hear an inner voice tell you that the wind can carry away troublesome thoughts and emotions. The voice says that for this, all you need to do is to take in a deep breath, and each time as you breathe out, say to yourself what troublesome thought or emotion you are releasing into the wind. So you take a deep breath, and as you breathe out, you say to yourself, "I release all of my fear into the wind." *(Pause)* You take another deep breath and as you breathe out, you say to yourself, "I release all of my guilt into the wind." *(Pause) (Repeat separately for anger, resentment, remorse, jealousy, doubt, despair, sorrow, etc., pausing after each.)*

You now feel that you are in a state of mental, emotional, and spiritual peace, cleansed of all troublesome thoughts and emotions. You give thanks to our Creator for this wonderful experience. *(Pause)*

You walk back through the forest on the winding path, stopping for a moment to smell the flowers, look up through the trees at the sky, and listen to the birds. *(Pause)* You leave the forest and its welcoming sign, get into your car, and drive away.

You may open your eyes when you wish. *(Pause)*
*(A variation on this meditation might be to replace the meadow with a pool of clear, warm water, deep and large enough for bathing. A troublesome thought or emotion is washed away with each "going under" in the water for a few seconds.)*

<u>Example 2</u>

Let us prepare ourselves for this meditation by relaxing comfortably in our chairs, with our hands apart on our laps and our feet flat on the floor. Now close your eyes and breathe slowly and deeply three times, in through your nose and out through your mouth.

*(Accompany the breathing exercise with "in through your nose and out through your mouth.")*

Imagine that you are sitting alone on a bench under a tall maple tree, on a warm spring day. The bench is beside a tranquil pond upon which two swans are slowly gliding back and forth, barely making a ripple in the water of the pond. The leaves on the tree are not yet in full bloom, allowing the warmth of the sun to come through its branches. High overhead a hawk floats lazily back and forth in the deep blue sky. *(Pause)* In this place of serenity you begin to feel close to God, and wonder, "Would God hear me if I pray?" But as you begin to say a prayer, you find that some concerns and emotions are blocking the way to finding the right words to say. *(Pause)*

You are startled by a soft, male voice coming from behind you, asking, "Would you mind if I sit on this bench with you?" You turn around and see a smiling young man in jogging clothes and slightly out of breath. "Yes," you reply. *(Pause)*

As the young man sits down on the bench, he introduces himself as Christopher, and you reply with your first name. You feel compelled to engage him in conversation, and as you engage in a dialogue with him soon realize that he is very concerned about your mental and spiritual wellbeing. "Who is this person?" you begin to wonder. *(Pause)*

After several minutes of chatting with Christopher, he suggests that you close your eyes, and in your mind ask him to remove any concerns or emotions that are bothering you. You are surprised by his unexpected suggestion, but your inner voice tells you to "Trust him." So with your eyes closed, you say to him in your mind, "Please remove my fear." *(Pause).* Then in your mind you say to him, "Please remove my guilt." *(Pause)* *(Repeat separately for anger, resentment, remorse, jealousy, doubt, despair, sorrow, etc., pausing after each.)*

# WE CAN HELP GOD HEAL US

Christopher softly asks, "How are you now?" You realize that your mind and spirit are experiencing a deep sense of peace and you reply, "Wonderful, thank you!" *(Pause)* As Christopher gets up to leave, he gently grasps your hands in his, and says, "Good, now you can freely talk with God." As he jogs into the distance, you feel ready and able to pray. *(Pause)*

You may open your eyes when you wish. *(Pause)*
*(A variation on this meditation might be to replace "Christopher" with "your guardian angel.")*

Example 3

Let us prepare ourselves for this meditation by relaxing comfortably in our chairs with our hands apart on our laps and our feet flat on the floor. Now close your eyes, and breathe slowly and deeply three times, in through your nose and out through your mouth. *(Accompany this exercise with, "in through your nose and out through your mouth.")*

Imagine that you are alone on a beach on a warm summer day, walking barefoot on a stretch of sand kept moist by small waves washing onto the shore. To your right the dark blue water stretches to the horizon, where it blends with the cloudless blue sky. To your left are small dunes of fine, rippled sand, capped by tall grass which is swaying in the gentle breeze. *(Pause)*

You stop and look at the water, sky and sand, and momentarily experience being at peace. *(Pause)* You ask yourself, "Why can't I feel this way all the time? *(Pause)* Almost immediately an inner voice replies: "Because your mind is cluttered with so many troublesome thoughts and emotions." *(Pause)* Then the voice tells you, "Go to the water's edge and write a thought or emotion that is bothering you in the moist sand, and let a wave come and wash it away from the beach and, in turn, your mind." *(Pause)*

You pick up a small, smooth stick, and kneel at the water's edge. As a wave recedes you write in the sand, "fear," which is washed away by the next wave. *(Pause)* Then you write "guilt," which is washed away by the next wave. *(Pause)* *(Repeat separately for anger, resentment, remorse, jealousy, doubt, despair, sorrow, etc., pausing after each.)*

When you have no other troublesome thought or emotion to write in the sand and be washed away, you realize that you are experiencing a deep sense of peace. You continue walking along the beach, enjoying its beauty. *(Pause)*

You may open your eyes when you wish.

(A variation of this meditation might be to write each troublesome thought or emotion in the sand of a dune, to be blown away by the wind.)

Example 4

Let us prepare ourselves for this meditation by relaxing comfortably in our chairs, with our hands apart on our laps and our feet flat on the floor. Now close your eyes and breathe slowly and deeply three times, in through your nose and out through your mouth. *(Accompany the breathing exercise with "in through your nose and out through your mouth.")*

Imagine a vertical beam of golden energy forming in the air above you, and after several seconds slowly extending downwards to gently touch the crown of your head. *(Pause)* Now the golden energy spreads and flows outwards and downwards over your entire body *(Pause)* Feel the pleasant warmth of the energy as it covers your head and neck, your shoulders, arms and hands, your chest and abdomen, your back, your pelvis, legs and feet, and finally passes through the soles of your feet into Mother Earth. *(Pause)*

You hear an inner voice invite you to release any troublesome thoughts or emotions into the golden energy flowing over you, to be

# WE CAN HELP GOD HEAL US

carried into the Earth. You do so, and say to yourself, "I release all of my fear." *(Pause)* Then you say to yourself, "I release all of my guilt." *(Pause) (Repeat separately for anger, resentment, remorse, jealousy, doubt, despair, sorrow, etc., pausing after each.)*

The golden energy seems to know when you have no more to troublesome thoughts or emotions to release into it. The energy slowly shrinks and flows upwards to the crown of your head, and becomes an ascending beam of golden energy which disappears in the space above you. *(Pause)* You feel mental, emotional and spiritual peace. *(Pause)*

You may open your eyes when you wish. *(Pause)*

<u>Example 5</u>

Let us prepare ourselves for this meditation by relaxing comfortably in our chairs with our hands apart on our laps and our feet flat on the floor. Now close your eyes, and breathe slowly and deeply three times, in through your nose and out through your mouth. *(Accompany the breathing exercise with "in through your nose and out through your mouth.")*

Imagine that you are with several of your friends, sitting around a campfire. After sharing several stories, everyone becomes quiet, gazing into the fire. *(Pause)* You feel the warmth of the fire, hear the crackling of the burning wood, and are entranced by multicolored flames rising to release golden sparks into the dark night air. *(Pause)* Soon you realize that you could be enjoying this moment more if your mind would be free of troublesome thoughts and emotions. You share this difficulty with your friends, and most say that they feel the same way. *(Pause)*

One of your friends suggests a way to rid the mind of troublesome thoughts and emotions. She hands a pencil and small pad of paper to each person around the fire. She suggests writing one troublesome thought or emotion at a time on the pad, gazing at the word or words for several seconds, and then tearing the paper off the pad and throwing it into the fire. You write "fear" on the pad, look at this word for several seconds, tear the paper off the pad, and throw it into the fire. *(Pause)* Then you write "guilt" on the pad, look at this word for several seconds, tear the paper off the pad, and throw it into the fire. *(Pause) (Repeat separately for anger, remorse, jealousy, doubt, despair, sorrow, etc., pausing after each.)*

When you have no more troublesome thoughts or emotions to be consumed by the fire, you realize that you are experiencing a deep sense of peace. You can now fully enjoy this wonderful moment with your friends around the fire. *(Pause)*

You may open your eyes when you wish. *(Pause)*

## Prayers for Healing

Lord, make me an instrument of your peace,
Where there is hatred, let me sow love.
Where there is injury, let me sow pardon.
Where there is discord, let me sow unity.
Where there is doubt, let me sow faith.
Where there is despair, let me sow hope.
Where there is sadness, let me sow joy.
Where there is darkness, let me sow light.
O Divine Master, grant that I may not so much seek
    to be consoled as to console.
To be understood, as to understand.
To be loved, as to love.
For it is in the giving, that we receive.
It is in the pardoning, that we are pardoned.
It is in dying, that we are born to eternal life.

Saint Francis of Assisi[97]

Lay your hands gently upon us,
let their touch render your peace,

# WE CAN HELP GOD HEAL US

let them bring your love and healing.
Lay your hands, gently lay your hands.

You were sent to free the broken-hearted,
You were sent to give sight to the blind,
You desire to heal all our illness.
Lay your hands, gently lay your hands.

Lord, we come to you through one another.
Lord, we come to you in all our need.
Lord, we come to you seeking wholeness,
Lay your hands, gently lay your hands.

                              Rita J. Donovan[84] (adapted)

This is a prayer for the illumination of the body
    the body of the earth
    which is our rock and breath
    the body of the self
        which is the shining
        eternal strand of
        the soul
    the body of material substance which
        is the ancient gentle
        temple of the spirit.
May you move your divine hand
across us in each of these planes,
allowing the earth
of our bodies
and the ether
of our souls
to become fit grand vessels
for your own and our own
illustrious light.

                              Daphne Rose Kingma[84]

# DOUGLAS E. BUSBY

O Christ of the road
    of the wounded
O Christ of the tears
    of the broken
In me and with me
    the needs of the world
Grant us our prayers
    of loving and hoping
Grant us our prayers
    of yearning and healing.

J. Philip Newell[98] (adapted)

Hear our prayers O Lord. You who are the giver of life and health: Send your blessing on all here present who seek healing in mind, body and spirit. We trust in you, Lord, who knows our hearts as we stand before you desiring wholeness.

Linda L. Smith[78]

O God, we humbly to ask you to heal those for whom we pray. Our spirits are fully open, ready to connect in love with you and each other to receive your timeless gift of spiritual healing.

Douglas Busby

We thank you, God of all Creation, for your love for us. As Jesus Christ healed and taught his disciples how to help you heal us, we come together for spiritual healing in his name. Please bless us at this time and place with the healing power of your Spirit to heal us and others for whom we pray.

Douglas Busby

Loving God, we come to you in our love for you and each other, to ask that you let us help you heal us with your healing energy. May our laying on of hands serve to channel this energy for spiritual healing.

Douglas Busby

# WE CAN HELP GOD HEAL US

All-powerful God, source of all healing, make those for whom we are to use the laying on of hands and pray for their spiritual healing fully aware of your presence with them. Open their eyes that they may see you; open their ears that they hear you; open their hearts that they may know your love. Cast the light of your Spirit upon them, so that they may be healed in body, mind, and spirit.

Douglas Busby

**Prayers of Thankfulness**

Loving God, we are deeply thankful that you have been with us for spiritual healing, and have provided your healing energy to those on whom we have laid our hands to channel this energy to them and prayed for their healing. We humbly ask that you continue to send them healing through the power of your Spirit.

Douglas Busby

O God, we are profoundly grateful for the healing that you have provided to those for whom we have prayed. We earnestly pray that you will continue to embrace them with your healing Spirit, as they continue to hope and pray for wholeness of body, mind, and spirit.

Douglas Busby

God of all love, we are profoundly thankful that you have heard our prayers and have blessed us with healing of body, mind, and spirit. We humbly ask that you will continue to provide healing to those on whom we have laid our hands while praying for their healing.

Douglas Busby

We thank you, O God, for blessing us with the healing energy of your Spirit. We ask that you to help us be constantly mindful of your unconditional love for us, and of your desire that we be whole in body, mind, and spirit.

Douglas Busby

## DOUGLAS E. BUSBY

**Parting Songs**
God be with you till we meet again[99]
By good counsels guide, uphold you,
With a shepherd's care enfold you:
God be with you till we meet again.
*Till we meet, till we meet,*
*till we meet at Jesus' feet;*
*till we meet, till we meet,*
*God be with you till we meet again.*

--------

God, dismiss us with your blessing;[100]
Fill our hearts with joy and peace;
Let us each your love possessing,
Give us still your healing grace;
Oh refresh us, oh refresh us,
traveling through this wilderness.

--------

God be with you, God be with you,[101]
God be with you till we meet again.
O God be with you, God be with you,
God be with you till we meet again.

--------

Blest be the tie that binds[102]
our hearts in Christian love;
The fellowship of kindred minds
is like to that above.

When we are called to part,
it gives us inward pain;
But we shall be joined in heart,
and hope to meet again.

# WE CAN HELP GOD HEAL US

Alleluia, alleluia, alleluia, alleluia,[103]
Alleluia, alleluia, alleluia, alleluia.

## Blessings

As we leave this place, we commend ourselves to God's everlasting care, ever mindful of God's healing presence in our lives.

Douglas Busby

Be assured of God's unceasing love.
God is always ready to hear us
God is always ready to heal us,
Whenever we ask God for healing.

Douglas Busby

May God our Creator,
the Source of all love,
the Source of all healing,
bless us with peace and joy,
now and always.

Douglas Busby

We have come together to follow Jesus' way of spiritual healing, with spiritual faith, compassion, prayer and the laying on of hands. May we continue to follow Jesus' footsteps in healing ministry by helping God heal us.

Douglas Busby

# References

1. Busby, D. E. (2007). *Coming together for spiritual healing*. West Conshohocken, PA: Infinity Publishing.
2. Busby, D. E. (2018). *Spirits can help God heal us*. Kindle Direct Publishing, book https://www.amazon.com/dp/1727856481, e-book https://www.amazon.com/dp/B07JLKTPQQ
3. Ackerknecht, E. H. (1982). *A Short History of Medicine*. Baltimore, MD: The John Hopkins University Press.
4. Magner, L. N. (1992). *A History of Medicine*. New York: Marcel Dekker, Inc.
5. Kelsey, M. (1995). *Healing and Christianity: A Classic Study* Minneapolis, MN: Augsburg Fortress.
6. Bakken, K. L. (2000). *The journey into God: healing and the Christian faith*. Minneapolis, MN: Augsburg Fortress.
7. Crenshaw, J. L. (1993). *Job,* in the HarperCollins Study Bible: New Revised Standard Version. New York, NY: HarperCollins Publishers.
8. Sanford, J. A., (1992). *Healing body and soul: the meaning of illness in the New Testament and in psychotherapy*. Louisville, KY: Westminster John Knox Press.
9. Bandstra, B. L. (1995). *Reading the Old Testament: an introduction to the Hebrew Bible*. New York, NY: Wadsworth Publishing Company.
10. Preuss, J. (1993). *Biblical and Talmudic medicine*, translated from German by F. Rosner. Northvale, NJ: Jason Aronson Inc.

11   Crossan, D. (1998). *The birth of Christianity: discovering what happened in the years immediately after the execution of Jesus.* San Francisco, CA: HarperCollins Publishers.

12   Borg, M. T., Wright, N. T. (1999). *The meaning of Jesus: two visions.* San Francisco, CA: HarperCollins Publishers.

13   Sussman, M. Sickness and Disease. In Freedman, D. N., Herion, G. A., Graf, D. F., Pleins, J. P., Beck, A. B. *Anchor Yale Bible Dictionary, Volume 6.* (1992). New York, NY: Doubleday & Company, Inc.

14   Nash, J. E., Kearns, S. C. J. (2019). *Leprosy: infectious disease.* https://www.britannica.com/science/leprosy.

15   Davies, S. L. (1995). *Jesus the healer: possession, trance, and the origin of Christianity.* New York, NY: The Continuum Publishing Company.

16   Harpur, T. (1994). *The uncommon touch: an investigation of spiritual healing.* Toronto, Ontario, Canada: McClellan & Stewart Inc.

17   Fiore, E. (1987). *The unquiet dead: a psychiatrist treats spirit possession.* Garden City, NY: Doubleday & Company, Inc.

18   MacNutt, F. (1995). *Deliverance from evil spirits: a practical manual.* Grand Rapids, MI: Chosen Books.

19   Sagan, S. (1997). *Entity possession: freeing the energy body of negative influences.* Rochester, VT: Destiny Books.

20   Key, H. C. (1986). *Medicine, miracle and magic in New Testament times.* New York, NY: Cambridge University Press.

21   Douglas-Klotz, N. (1990). *Prayers of the cosmos: meditations on the Aramaic words of Jesus.* San Francisco, CA: HarperCollins Publishers.

22 Roth, R., with P. Occhiogrosso. (1997). *The healing path of prayer: a modern mystic's guide to spiritual power*. New York, NY; Three Rivers Press.

23 Wimber, J., Springer, K. (1987). *Power healing*. New York, NY: HarperCollins Publishers.

24 Evans, A, R. (1999). *The healing church: practical programs for healing ministries*. Cleveland, OH: United Church Press.

25 International Commission on English in the Liturgy. (1983). *Pastoral care of the sick: rites of anointing and viaticum*. New York, NY: Roman Catholic Book Publishing.

26 Cranston, R. (1988). *The miracle of Lourdes: updated and expanded by the medical bureau of Lourdes*. New York, NY: Image Books.

27 Flach, F. (2000). *Faith, healing, and miracles*. New York, NY: Hatherleigh Press.

28 Zuendel, F. (2000). *The awakening: one man's battle with darkness*. Farmington, PA: Plough Publishing House.

29 Kuhlman, K. (1974). *Nothing is impossible with God*. Alachua, FL: Bridge-Logos.

30 Harrell, D. E., Jr. (1975). *All things are possible: the healing and charismatic revivals in modern America*. Bloomington, IN: Indiana University Press.

31 Roberts, O. (1995). *Expect a miracle: my life and ministry; an autobiography*. Nashville, TN: Thomas Nelson Publishers.

32 Goldsmith, J. (1959). *The art of spiritual healing*. San Francisco, CA: HarperCollins Publishers.

33 Sanford, A. (1947). *The healing light*. Austin, MN: Macalester Park Publishing Company.

34  Sanford, A. (1972). *Sealed orders: autobiography of Agnes Sanford.* Alachua, FL: Bridge-Logos.

35  Worrall, A. A., Worrall, O. (1985). *The gift of healing: a personal story of spiritual therapy.* Columbus, OH: Ariel Press.

36  MacNutt, F. (1999). *Healing.* Notre Dame, IN: Ave Maria Press.

37  Roth, R., with P. Occhiogrosso. (1999). *Prayer and the five stages of healing.* Carlsbad, CA: Hay House, Inc.

38  The Church of England. (1795). *The Book of Common Prayer and administration of the sacraments and other rites and ceremonies according to the Church of England.* London, England: Clarendon Press.

39  The Episcopal Church. (1976). *The Book of Common Prayer and administration of the sacraments and other rites and ceremonies of the Church.* New York, NY: Church Publishing Incorporated.

40  Benson, H. (1996). *Timeless healing: the power and biology of belief.* New York, NY: Fireside.

41  Braden, G. (2004). *The God code: the secret of our past, the promise of our future.* Carlsbad, CA: Hay House, Inc.

42  Keck, L. R. (2002). *Healing as a sacred path: a personal story of personal medical and spiritual transformation.* West Chester, PA: Chrysalis Books.

43  Tillich, P. (1959). *Theology of culture.* New York, NY: Oxford University Press.

44  Pert, C. B. (1997). *Molecules of emotion: the science of mind-body medicine.* New York, NY: Touchstone.

45  Dossey, L. (1999). *Reinventing medicine; beyond mind-body to a new era of healing.* San Francisco, CA: HarperCollins Publishers.

46  Droege, T. A. (1991). *The faith factor in healing.* Philadelphia, PA: Trinity Press International.

47  Levin, J. (2001). *God, faith and health: exploring the spirituality-healing connection.* New York, NY: John Wiley & Sons, Inc.

48  Koenig, H. G. (1997). *Is religion good for your health? The effects of religion on physical and mental health.* New York, NY: Haworth Pastoral Press.

49  Norberg, T., Webber, R. D. (1998). *Stretch out your hand: exploring healing prayer.* Nashville, TN: Upper Room Books.

50  Davies, G. (2017). *Mindfulness, empathy and compassion.* https://mind-lab.com/mindfulness-empathy-compassion.

51  Simon-Thomas, E. R. (2012).*Three insights from the cutting edge of compassion research.* https://greatergood.berkeley.edu/article/item/three_insights_from_the_cutting_edge_of_compassion_research

52  Epperly, B. G. (2001). *God's touch: faith, wholeness, and the healing miracles of Jesus.* Louisville, KY: Westminster John Knox Press.

53  Targ, R., Katra, J. (1999). *Miracles of the mind: exploring nonlocal consciousness and spiritual healing.* Novato, CA: New World Library.

54  Zahourek, R. P. (2012). *Healing through the lens of intentionality.* Holist Nurs Pract 26:6-21.

55  Hirshberg, C., Barasch, M. I. (1995). *Remarkable recovery: what remarkable healings tell us about getting well and staying well.* New York, NY: Riverhead Books.

56  Pruitt, J. (1999). *Healed by prayer.* New York, NY: Avon Books.

57  Wakefield, D. (1995). *The miraculous things that happen to ordinary people.* New York, NY: HarperCollins Publishers.

58  Pearsall, P. K. (2001). *On a wish and a prayer: healing through distant intentionality.* Hawaii Med. J. 60:255-256.

59  Radin, D., Schlitz, M., Baur, C. (2015). *Distant healing intention therapies: an overview of the scientific evidence.* Glob Adv Health Med 4(Suppl):67-71.

60  Schlitz, M., Braud, W. (1997). *Distant intentionality and healing: assessing the evidence.* Altern Ther Health Med 3:62-73.

61  Jonas, W. B., Crawford, C. C. (2003). *Science and spiritual healing: a critical review of spiritual healing, "energy medicine," and intentionality.* Alt Ther Health Med 9:56-61.

62  Masters K. S., Spielmans, G. I., Goodson, J. T. (2006). *Are there demonstrable effects of distant intercessory prayer? A meta-analytic review.* Ann Behav Med 32:21-26.

63  Walach, H., Bosch, H., Lewith, G., et al. (2008). *Effectiveness of distant healing for patients with chronic fatigue syndrome: a randomized controlled partially blinded trial (EUHEALS).* Psychother Psychosom 77:158-66.

64  Byrd, R. C. (1988). *Positive therapeutic effects of intercessory prayer in a coronary care unit population.* South Med J 81:826-829.

65  Harris, W. S., Gowda, M., Kolb, J. W., et al. (1999). *A randomized, controlled trial of the effects of remote, intercessory prayer on outcomes in patients admitted to the coronary care unit.* Arch Intern Med 159:2273-2278.

66  Aviles, J. M., Whelan, S. E., Hernke, D. E., et al. (2001). *Intercessory prayer and cardiovascular disease progression in a coronary care unit population: a randomized controlled trial.* Mayo Clin Proc 76:1192-1198.

67  Krucoff, M. W., Crater, S. W., Gallup, D., et al. (2005). *Music, imagery, touch, and prayer as adjuncts to interventional cardiac*

care: the Monitoring and Actualisation of Noetic Trainings (MANTRA) II randomized study. Lancet 366:211-217.

68  Benson, H., Dusek, J. A., Sherwood, J. B., et al. (2006). *Study of the Therapeutic Effects of Intercessory Prayer (STEP) in cardiac bypass patients: a multicenter randomized trial of uncertainty and certainty in receiving intercessory prayer.* Am Heart J 151:934-942.

69  Fiand, B. (1999). *Prayer and the quest for healing: our personal transformation and cosmic responsibility.* New York, NY: The Crossroad Publishing Company.

70  Ryan, B. S. (2001). *Healing prayer; spiritual pathways to health and wellness.* Cincinnati, OH: St. Anthony Messenger Press.

71  MacNutt, F. (1977). *The power to heal.* Notre Dame, IN; Ave Maria Press.

72  Connelly, D. (1994). *Angels around us: what the Bible really says.* Downers Grove, IL: InterVarsity Press.

73  Giudici, M., P. (1993). *The angels: spiritual and exegetical notes* (translated from the Italian by E. C. Lane). New York, NY: Alba House.

74  Smith, L., L. (2000). *Called into healing: reclaiming our Judeo-Christian legacy of healing touch.* Arvada, CO: HTSM Press.

75  Brennan, B. A. (1987). *Hands of light: a guide to healing through the human energy field.* New York, NY: Bantam Press.

76  Eden, D., with D. Feinstein. (1999). *Energy medicine.* New York, NY: Jeremy P. Tarcher.

77  Gerber, R. (2000). *Vibrational medicine for the 21st century: the complete guide to energy healing and spiritual transformation.* New York, NY: HarperCollins Publishers.

78  Keng, S.-L. , Smoski, M. L., Robins C. J. (2011). *Effects of mindfulness on psychological health: a review of empiric studies.* Clin Psychol Rev 31:1041-1056.

79  Schmidt, S. (2004). *Mindfulness and healing intention: concepts, practice, and research evaluation.* J Altern Complement Med 10 Suppl 1:S7-14.

80  Roberts, E, Amidon, E., editors. (1996). *Life prayers from around the world: 365 prayers, blessings, and affirmations to celebrate the human journey.* San Francisco, CA: HarperCollins Publishers. Reprinted with the permission of Elizabeth Roberts and Elias Roberts Amidon.

81  *Spirit of the Living God.* The words and music are by Daniel Iverson (1926). The words and music are in the public domain.

82  Kirvan, J. (1996). *Let nothing disturb you: a journey to the center of the soul with Teresa of Avila.* Notre Dame, IN; Ave Maria Press. Excerpted

83  Oman, M., editor. (1997). *Prayers for healing: 365 blessings, poems, and meditations from around the world.* Berkeley, CA: Conari Press. Excerpted.

84  Oman, M., editor. (1997). *Prayers for healing: 365 blessings, poems, and meditations from around the world.* Berkeley, CA: Conari Press. Reprinted with the permission of Jim Cohn.

85  Harris, B. (2003). *Something at the center.* New York, NY: iUniverse Publishing. Reprinted with the permission of Barry Harris.

86  Oman, M., editor. (1997). *Prayers for healing: 365 blessings, poems, and meditations from around the world.* Berkeley, CA: Conari Press. Reprinted with the permission of Dawna Markova.

# WE CAN HELP GOD HEAL US

87 Oman, M., editor. (1997). *Prayers for healing: 365 blessings, poems, and meditations from around the world.* Berkeley, CA: Conari Press. Reprinted with the permission of the Office of Information, Bahá'í International Community.

88 Verses 1 and 2 of *All People That on Earth Do Dwell.* Words by William Kethe (1561). The music ("Old Hundredth") is attributed to Louis Bourgeois (1551). The words and music are in the public domain.

89 Verse 1 of *Precious Lord, Take My Hand.* The words and music are by Thomas A. Dorsey (1932). The words are reprinted and the music can be used with the permission of Unichapell Music Inc.

90 Verses 1 and 3 of *Breathe on Me, Breath of God.* The words are by Edwin Hatch (1878) and music is by Robert Jackson (1888). The words and music are in the public domain.

91 Verses 1 and 3 of *Amazing Grace.* The original words are by John Newton (1779) and music is of the early Protestant Hymn, "New Britain," which was subsequently arranged by Edwin O. Excell (1900). The words and music are in the public domain.

92 Verse 1 of *This Little Light of Mine.* The words and music are of an African-American spiritual. The words and music are in the public domain.

93 Verses 1 and 3 of *O Holy Spirit, Root of Life.* The words are by Jean Janzen, based on the writings of Hildegard of Bingen (1098-1179). The music is from the Trier Manuscript (1852), adapted by Michael Praetorius (1609). The words are reprinted with the permission of Jean Janzen. The music is in the public domain.

94 Verses 1 and 3 of *For the Beauty of the Earth.* The original words are by Folliott S. Pierpoint (1864) and the music is by Conrad Kocher (1838). The words and music are in the public domain.

95   *Open My Eyes, That I May See.* The words and music are by Clara H. Scott (1895). The words and music are in the public domain.

96   Verses 1 and 3 of *Come Forth, O Love Divine.* The original words were in Italian by Bianco da Siena (d. 1434), and translated into English by Richard F. Littledale (1867). The music is by Ralph Vaughan Williams (1906). The words are in the public domain.

97   Allen, P. M., Allen, J. d. (1996). *Francis of Assisi's Canticle of the Creatures: a modern spiritual path.* New York, NY: Continuum International Publishing Group. Reprinted with the permission of the publisher.

98   Newell, J. P. (1997). *Celtic Prayers from Iona.* Nahwah, NJ; Paulist Press. Reprinted with the permission of the Paulist Press.

99   Verse 1 of *God Be with You Till We Meet Again.* The original words were by Jeremiah E. Rankin (1880) and the music is by William G. Tomer (1880). The words and music are in the public domain.

100  Verse 1 of *God, Dismiss Us with Your Blessing (adapted).* The original words are attributed to John Fawcett (1773) and the music to an 18th Century Sicilian melody published in The European Magazine Review (1792). The words and music are in the public domain.

101  *God Be with You.* The words and music are by Thomas A. Dorsey and Artelia W. Hutchins (1940). The words are reprinted and the music can be used with the permission of Unichapell Music Inc.

102  *Blest Be the Tie That Binds.* The words are by John Fawcett (1872) and the music is by Johann G. Nägeli (1828) and arranged by Lowell Mason (1845). The words and music are in the public domain.

103  *Alleluia.* This is the traditional eight-fold Alleluia. The music is copyright by various composers.

# APPENDIX A
# Jesus and Spiritual Healing

(The spiritual healing events listed below are in the order described in each of the Gospels, first in the oldest Gospel of Mark, and then in Matthew, Luke, and John.)

| Health Conditions | Sources | What Jesus Did |
|---|---|---|
| A man possessed by an evil spirit | Mk 1:23-26<br>Lk 4:33-35 | But Jesus rebuked him saying, "Be silent, and come out of him!" (Mk 1:25). |
| Peter's mother-in-law with a fever | Mk 1:29-34<br>Mt 8:14-15<br>Lk 4:38-39 | Now Simon's mother-in-law was in bed with a fever, and they told him about her at once. He came and took her by the hand and lifted her up. Then the fever left her, and she began to serve them (Mk 1:30, 31). |
| People sick or possessed by demons | Mk 1:32-34<br>Mt 8:16<br>Lk 4:40-41 | That evening, at sundown, they brought to him all who were sick or possessed with demons. And the whole city was gathered around the door. And he cured many who were sick with various diseases, and cast out many demons; and he would not permit the demons to speak, because they knew him (Mk 1:32-34). |
| People possessed by demons | Mk 1:39 | And he went throughout Galilee, proclaiming the message in their synagogues and casting out demons (Mk 1:39). |
| A man with leprosy | Mk 1:40-42<br>Mt 8:2, 3<br>Lk 5:12-13 | A leper came to him, and kneeling he said to him, "If you choose, you can make me clean." Moved with pity, Jesus stretched out his hand and touched him, and said to him, "I do choose. Be made clean!" Immediately the leprosy left him, and he was made clean (Mk 1:40-42). |
| A man bedridden by paralysis | Mk 2:10-12<br>Mt 9:2-7<br>Lk 5:17-25 | "But so you know that the Son of Man has authority on earth to forgive sins - he said to the paralytic - "I say to you, stand up, take your mat and go to your home." And he stood up, and immediately took the mat and went out before all of them; so that they |

| | | |
|---|---|---|
| | | were all amazed and glorified God, saying, "we have never seen anything like this!" (Mk 2:10-12). |
| A man with a withered hand | Mk 3:1-5<br>Mt 12:9-13<br>Lk 6:6-10 | Again he entered the synagogue, and a man was there who had a withered hand ... And he said to the man who had the withered hand, "Come forward" ... and "Stretch out your hand"... He stretched it out, and his hand was restored (Mk 3:3, 5). |
| People with diseases | Mk 3:9-11<br>Mt 12:15 | He told his disciples to have a boat ready for him because of the crowd, so that they would not crush him; for he had cured many, so that all who had diseases pressed upon him to touch him. Whenever the unclean spirits saw him, they fell down before him and shouted, "You are the Son of God"(Mk 3:9-11). |
| A man possessed by unclean spirits | Mk 5:2-13<br>Mt 8:28-32<br>Lk 8:27-33 | And when he had stepped out of the boat, immediately a man out of the tombs with an unclean spirit met him. ... For he had said to him, "Come out of the man, you unclean spirit!" ... He begged him earnestly not to send them out of the country. Now there on the hillside a great herd of swine was feeding; and the unclean spirits begged him, "Send us into the swine; let us enter them." So he gave them permission. And the unclean spirits came out and entered the swine; and the herd , numbering about two thousand, rushed down the steep bank into the sea, and were drowned in the sea (Mk 5:2, 8, 10-13). |
| A little daughter at the point of death | Mk 5:22, 23, 40-42<br>Mt 9:18-24<br>Lk 8:41-55 | Then one of the leaders of the synagogue named Jairus came, fell at his feet and begged him repeatedly, My little daughter is at the point of death. Come and lay your hands on her, so that she may be made well, and live."... Then he put them all outside, and took the child's father and mother and those who were with him, and went in where the child was. |

# WE CAN HELP GOD HEAL US

| | | |
|---|---|---|
| | | He took her by the hand and said to her, her, "Talitha cum," which means, "Little girl, get up!" And immediately the girl got up and began to walk about (she was 12 years of age) (Mk 5:22, 23, 40-42). |
| A woman with gynecological bleeding | Mk 5:25-29<br>Mt 9:20-22<br>Lk 8:43-48 | Now there was a woman who had been suffering from hemorrhages for twelve years. She had endured much under many physicians, and had spent all that she had; and she was no better, but rather grew worse. She had heard about Jesus, and came up behind him in the crowd and touched his cloak, for she said, "If I but touch his clothes, I will be made well." Immediately her hemorrhage stopped; and she felt in her body that she was healed of her disease. ... He said to her, "Daughter, your faith has made you well; go in peace, and be healed of your disease" (Mk 5:25-29, 34). |
| People who were sick | Mk 6:54-56<br>Mt 14:35, 36 | When they got out of the boat, people at once recognized him, and rushed about that whole region and began to bring the sick on mats to wherever they heard he was. And wherever he went, into villages or cities or farms, they laid the sick in the market-places, and begged him that they might touch even the fringe of his cloak; and all who touched it were healed (Mk 6 54-56). |
| A daughter possessed by an unclean spirit | Mk 7:25-30<br>Mt 15:22-28 | Yet he could not escape notice, but a woman whose little daughter had an unclean spirit immediately heard about him, and she came and bowed down at his feet. Now the woman was a Gentile, of Syrophoenician origin. She begged him to cast the demon out of her daughter. He said to her, "Let the children be fed first, for it is not fair to take the children's food and |

| | | |
|---|---|---|
| | | throw it to the dogs." But she answered him, "Sir, even the dogs throw it to the dogs." under the table eat the children's crumbs." Then he said to her, "For saying that, you may go – the demon has left your daughter." So she went home, found the child lying on the bed, and the demon gone (Mk 7:25-30). |
| A man with deafness and a speech impediment | Mk 7:32-35 | They brought him to a deaf man who had an impediment in his speech; and they begged him to lay his hand upon him. He took him aside in private, away from the crowd, and put his fingers into his ears, and he spat and touched his tongue. Then looking up to heaven, he sighed and said to him, "Ephphatha," that is, "Be opened." And immediately his ears were opened, his tongue was released, and he spoke plainly (Mk 7:32-35). |
| A man with blindness | Mk 8:22-26 | They came to Bethsaida. Some people brought a blind man to him and begged him to touch him. He took the blind man by the hand and led him out of the village; and when he had put saliva on his eyes and laid his hands on him, he asked him, "Can you see anything?" And the man looked up and said, "I can see people, but they look like trees, walking." Then Jesus laid his hands on his eyes again; and he looked intently and his sight was restored, and he saw everything clearly (Mk 8:22-26). |
| A boy possessed by an evil spirit causing muteness and convulsions | Mk 9:17-29 Mt 7:14-20 Lk 9:38-42 | Someone from the crowd answered him, "Teacher I brought you my son; he has a spirit that makes him unable to speak; and whenever it seizes him, it dashes him down; and he foams and grinds his teeth and becomes rigid; and I asked your disciples to cast it out, but they could not do so." ... Jesus said to him, "If you are able! - All |

# WE CAN HELP GOD HEAL US

| | | |
|---|---|---|
| | | things can be done for the one who believes." Immediately the father of the child cried out, "I believe; help my unbelief!" When Jesus saw that a crowd came running together, he rebuked the unclean spirit, saying to it, "You spirit that keeps this boy from speaking and hearing, I command you, come out of him, and never enter him again!" After crying out and convulsing him terribly, it came out, and the boy was like a corpse, so that most of them said, "He is dead." But Jesus took him by the hand and lifted him up, and he was able to stand. When he had entered the house, his disciples asked him privately, "Why could we not cast it out?" He said to them, "This kind can only come out through prayer "(Mk 9:17, 18, 23-29) |
| A man with blindness | Mk 10:46-52<br>Lk 18:35-43 | They came to Jericho. As he and his disciples, and a large crowd were leaving Jericho, Bartimaeus son of Timaeus, a blind beggar, was sitting by the roadside. ... Jesus stood still and said, "Call him here." And they called the blind man, saying to him, "Take heart; get up, he is calling you. " So throwing off his cloak, he sprang up and came to Jesus. Then Jesus said to him, "What do you want me to do for you?' The blind man said to him, My teacher, let me see again." Jesus said to him, "Go; your faith has made you well." Immediately he regained his sight and followed him on the way (Mk 10:46, 49-52). |
| People who were afflicted with every disease and every sickness, including various diseases and pains, demoniacs, epileptics and paralytics | Mt 4:23-24<br>Lk 6:17-20 | Jesus went throughout Galilee, teaching in their synagogues and proclaiming the good news of the kingdom and curing every disease and every sickness among the people. So his fame spread throughout all Syria, |

|  |  | and they brought to him all the sick, those who were afflicted with various diseases and pains, demoniacs, epileptics, and paralytics, and he cured them (Mt 6:23-24). |
| --- | --- | --- |
| A man with leprosy | Mt 8:1-3 | When Jesus had come down from the mountain, great crowds followed him; and there was a leper who came to him and knelt before him, saying, "Lord, if you choose, you can make me clean" He stretched out his hand and touched him, saying, "I do choose. Be made clean." Immediately his leprosy was cleansed (Mt 8:1-3). |
| A centurion's servant with paralysis | Mt 8:5-13 | When he entered Capernaum, a centurion came to him, appealing to him and saying, "Lord, my servant is lying at home paralyzed, in terrible distress." And he said to him, "I will come and cure him." The centurion answered, "Lord, I am not worthy to have you come under my roof; but only speak the word, and my servant will be healed." ... And to the centurion Jesus said, "Go; let it be done for you according to your faith." And the servant was healed in that hour. (Mt 8:5-8, 13). |
| Two men who were blind | Mt 9:28-30 | When he entered the house, the blind men came to him; and Jesus said to them, "Do you believe that I am able to do this?" They said to him, "Yes, Lord." Then he touched their eyes and said, "According to your faith let it be done to you." And their eyes were opened (Mt 9:28-30). |
| A person who was a demoniac and mute | Mt 9:32, 33 | After they had gone away, a demoniac who was mute was brought to him. And when the demon had been cast out, the one who had been mute spoke; and the crowds were amazed and said, "Never has anything like this been seen in Israel" (Mt 9:32, 33). |

# WE CAN HELP GOD HEAL US

| People with disease and sickness | Mt 9:35-37 | Then Jesus went about all the cities and villages, teaching in their synagogues, and proclaiming the good news of the kingdom, and curing every disease and every sickness. When he saw the crowds, he had compassion for them, because they were harassed and helpless, like sheep without a shepherd (Mt 9:35-37). |
|---|---|---|
| A man who was a demoniac, blind, and mute | Mt 12:22<br>Lk 11:14 | Then they brought to him a demoniac who was blind and mute; and he cured him, so that the one who had been mute could speak and see (Mt 12:22). |
| A great crowd with people who were sick | Mt 14:14<br>Lk 9:11<br>Jn 6:2 | When he went ashore, he saw a great crowd; and he had compassion for them and cured their sick (Mt .14:14). |
| Great crowds which brought to him people who were lame, maimed, blind, mute, and many others | Mt 15:30, 31 | Great crowds came to him, bringing with them the lame, the maimed, the blind, the mute, and many others. They put them at his feet, and he cured them, so that the crowd was amazed when they saw the mute speaking, the maimed whole, the lame walking, and the blind seeing. And they praised the God of Israel (Mt 15: 30, 31). |
| Large crowds, presumably with people with various medical conditions | Mt 19:2 | Large crowds followed him, and he cured them there (Mt 19:2). |
| Two men who were blind | Mt 20:29-34 | As they were leaving Jericho, a large crowd followed him. There were two blind men sitting by the roadside. When they heard that Jesus was passing by, they shouted, "Lord, have mercy on us, Son of David!" ... Jesus stood still and called them, saying, "What do you want me to do for you?" They said to him, "Lord, let our eyes be opened." Moved with compassion, Jesus touched their eyes. Immediately they regained their sight |

|  |  | and followed him (Mt 30:29, 30, 32-34). |
| --- | --- | --- |
| People who were blind and lame | Mt 21:14 | The blind and the lame came to him in the temple, and he cured them (Mt:21:14). |
| Many crowds with people with diseases. | Lk 5:15 | But now more than ever the word about Jesus spread abroad; many crowds would gather to hear him and to be cured of their diseases (Lk 5:15). |
| A widow's son who had died | Lk 7:11-15 | Soon afterwards he went to a town called Nain, and his disciples and a large crowd went with him. As he approached the gate of the town, a man who had died was being carried out. He was his mother's only son, and she was a widow; and with her was a large crowd from the town. When the Lord saw her, he had compassion for her and said to her, "Do not weep." Then he came forward and touched the bier, and the bearers stood still. And he said, "Young man, I say to you, rise!" The dead man sat up and began to speak, and Jesus gave him to his mother (Lk 7:11-15). |
| A woman crippled by a spirit | Lk 13:10-13 | Now he was teaching in one of the synagogues on the sabbath. And just then there appeared a woman with a spirit that had crippled her for eighteen years. She was bent over and was quite unable to stand up straight. When Jesus saw her, he called her over and said, "Woman, you are set free from your ailment." When he laid his hands on her, immediately she stood up straight and began praising God (Lk 13:10-13). |
| A man with dropsy | Lk. 14:1-4 | On one occasion when Jesus was going to the house of a leader of the Pharisees to eat a meal on the sabbath, they were watching him closely. Just then, in front of him, there was a man who had dropsy. And |

|   |   | Jesus asked the lawyers and Pharisees, "Is it lawful to cure people on the sabbath, or not?" But they were silent. So Jesus took him and healed him, and sent him away (Lk 14:1-4). |
|---|---|---|
| Ten people with leprosy | Lk 17:12-19 | As he entered a village, ten lepers approached him. Keeping their distance, they called out, saying, "Jesus, Master, have mercy on us!" When he saw them, he said to them, "Go and show yourselves to the priests." And as they went, they were made clean. Then one of them, when he saw that he was healed, turned back, praising God with a loud voice. He prostrated himself at Jesus' feet and thanked him. And he was a Samaritan. Then Jesus asked, "Were not ten made clean? But the other nine, where are they? Was none of them found to return and give praise to God except this foreigner?" Then he said to him, "Get up and go on your way; your faith has made you well" (Lk 17:12-19). |
| A slave with a severed ear | Lk 22:49-51 | When those who were around him saw what was coming, they asked, "Lord, should we strike with the sword?" Then one of them struck the slave of the high priest and cut off his right ear. But Jesus said, "No more of this!" And he touched his ear and healed him (Lk 22:49-51). |
| Little boy who was ill at the point of death | Jn 4:46-53 | Now there was a royal official whose son lay ill in Capernaum. When he heard that Jesus had come from Judea to Galilee, he went and begged him to come down and heal his son, for he was at the point of death. Then Jesus said to him, "Unless you see signs and wonders you will not believe." The official said to him, "Sir, come down |

|   |   |   |
|---|---|---|
|   |   | before my little boy dies." Jesus said to him, "Go; your son will live." The man believed the word that Jesus spoke to him and started on his way. As he was going down, his slaves met him and told him that his child was alive. So he asked them the hour when he began to recover, and they said to him, "Yesterday at one in the afternoon the fever left him." The father realized that this was the hour when Jesus had said to him, "Your son will live." So he himself believed, along with his whole household (Jn 4:46-53). |
| A man who had an illness making him unable to walk for 38 years | Jn 5:2-9 | Now in Jerusalem by the Sheep Gate there is a pool, called in Hebrew Bethzatha, which has five porticoes. In these lay many invalids - blind, lame, and paralyzed. One man was there who had been ill for thirty-eight years. When Jesus saw him lying there and knew that he had been there a long time, he said to him, "Do you want to be made well?" The sick man answered him, "Sir, I have no one to put me into the pool when the water is stirred up; and while I am making my way, someone else steps down ahead of me." Jesus said to him, "Stand up, take your mat and walk" At once the man was made well, and he took up his mat and began to walk (Jn 5:2-9). |
| A man who was born blind | Jn 9:1-7 | As he walked along, he saw a man blind from birth. His disciples asked him, "Rabbi, who sinned, this man or his parents, that he was born blind?" Jesus answered, "Neither this man nor his parents sinned; he was born blind so that God's works might be revealed in him." ... When he had said this, he spat on the ground and made mud with the saliva and spread the mud on |

| | | |
|---|---|---|
| | | the man's eyes, saying to him, "Go, wash in the pool of Siloam" (which means Sent). Then he went and washed and came back able to see (Jn 9:1-3, 6, 7). |
| Death of a man from an illness | Jn. 11:38-44 | Then Jesus, again greatly disturbed, came to the tomb. It was a cave, and a stone was lying against it. Jesus said, "Take away the stone." Martha, the sister of the dead man, said to him, "Lord, already there is a stench because he has been dead for four days." Jesus said to her, "Did I not tell you that if you believed, you would see the glory of God?" So they took away the stone. And Jesus looked upwards and said, "Father, I thank you for having heard me. I knew that you always hear me, but I have said this for the sake of the crowd standing here, so that they may believe that you sent me." When he had said this, he cried with a loud voice, "Lazarus, come out!" The dead man came out, his hands and feet bound with strips of cloth, and his face wrapped in a cloth. Jesus said to them, "'Unbind him, and let him go" (Jn 11:38-44). |

# APPENDIX B
# Jesus' Followers and Spiritual Healing

| Health Conditions | Sources | What Jesus' Followers Did |
|---|---|---|
| A man who was lame from birth | Acts 3:1-8 | One day Peter and John were going up to the temple at the hour of prayer, at three o'clock in the afternoon. And a man lame from birth was being carried in. People would lay him daily at the gate of the temple called the Beautiful Gate so that he could ask for alms from those entering the temple. When he saw Peter and John about to go into the temple, he asked them for alms. Peter looked intently at him, as did John, and said, "Look at us." And he fixed his attention on them, expecting to receive something from them. But Peter said, "I have no silver or gold, but what I have I give you; in the name of Jesus Christ of Nazareth, stand up and walk." And he took him by the right hand and raised him up; and immediately his feet and ankles were made strong. Jumping up, he stood and began to walk, and he entered the temple with them, walking and leaping and praising God (Acts 3:1-8). |
| People who were sick or possessed by unclean spirits | Acts 5:14, 15 | Yet more than ever believers were added to the Lord, great numbers of both men and women, so that they even carried out the sick into the streets, and laid them on cots and mats, in order that Peter's shadow might fall on some of them as he came by (5:14, 15). |
| People who were sick or tormented by unclean spirits | Acts 5:16 | A great number of people would also gather from the towns around Jerusalem, bringing the sick and those tormented by unclean spirits, and they were all cured (Acts 5:16). |
| People who were possessed by unclean spirits, or paralyzed or lame | Acts 8:6, 7 | The crowds with one accord listened eagerly to what was said by Philip, hearing and seeing the signs that he |

# WE CAN HELP GOD HEAL US

| | | |
|---|---|---|
| | | did, for unclean spirits, crying with loud shrieks, came out of many who were possessed; and many others who were paralyzed or lame were cured (Acts 8:6, 7). |
| Saul (before becoming the Apostle Paul) who had become blind | Acts 9:17, 18 | So Ananias went and entered the house. He laid his hands on Saul and said, "Brother Saul, the Lord Jesus, who appeared to you on your way here, has sent me so that you may regain your sight and be filled with the Holy Spirit." And immediately something like scales fell from his eyes, and his sight was restored (Acts 9:17, 18). |
| A man who had been paralyzed for eight years | Acts 9:32-34 | Now as Peter went here and there among all the believers, he came down also to the saints living in Lydda. There he found a man named Aeneas, who had been bedridden for eight years, for he was paralyzed. Peter said to him, "Aeneas, Jesus Christ heals you; get up and make your bed!" And immediately he got up (Acts 9:32-34). |
| A woman who became ill and died | Acts 9:36-41 | Now in Joppa there was a disciple whose name was Tabitha, which in Greek is Dorcas. She was devoted to good works and acts of charity. At that time she became ill and died. When they had washed her, they laid her in a room upstairs. Since Lydda was near Joppa, the disciples, who heard that Peter was there, sent two men to him with the request, "Please come to us without delay." So Peter got up and went with them; and when he arrived, they took him to the room upstairs. All the widows stood beside him, weeping and showing tunics and other clothing that Dorcas had made while she was with them. Peter put all of them outside, and then he knelt down and prayed. He turned to the body and said, "Tabitha, get up." Then she opened her eyes, and seeing Peter, she sat up. He gave her his hand and helped her up. Then calling the saints |

| | | and widows, he showed her to be alive (Acts 9:36-41). |
|---|---|---|
| A man who had been crippled since birth | Acts 14:8-10 | In Lystra there was a man sitting who could not use his feet and had never walked, for he had been crippled from birth. He listened to Paul as he was speaking. And Paul, looking at him intently and seeing that he had faith to be healed, said in a loud voice, "Stand upright on your feet." And the man sprang up and began to walk (Acts 14:8-10). |
| A slave girl who was possessed by a spirit | Acts 16:16-18 | ... we met a slave-girl who had a spirit of divination and brought her owners a great deal of money by fortune-telling. While she followed Paul and us, she would cry out, "These men are slaves of the Most High God, who proclaim to you a way of salvation." She kept doing this for many days. But Paul, very much annoyed, turned and said to the spirit, "I order you in the name of Jesus Christ to come out of her." And it came out that very hour (Acts 16:16-18). |
| Persons who were sick with diseases and evil spirit possessions | Acts 19:12 | God did extraordinary miracles through Paul, so that when the handkerchiefs or aprons that had touched his skin were brought to the sick, their diseases left them, and the evil spirits came out of them (Acts 19:12). |
| A young man who died in a fall | Acts 20:9, 10 | A young man named Eutychus, who was sitting in the window, began to sink off into a deep sleep while Paul talked still longer. Overcome by sleep, he fell to the ground three floors below and was picked up dead. But Paul went down, and bending over him took him in his arms, and said, "Do not be alarmed, for his life is in him" (Acts 20:9, 10). |
| A man who was sick in bed with a fever and dysentery | Acts 28:7, 8 | Now in the neighborhood of that place were lands belonging to the leading man of the island, named Publius, who received us and entertained us hospitably for three days. It so |

# WE CAN HELP GOD HEAL US

| | | |
|---|---|---|
| | | *happened that the father of Publius lay sick in bed with fever and dysentery. Paul visited him and cured him by praying and putting his hands on him (Acts 28:7, 8).* |
| (See above) People who had diseases | Acts 28:9 | *After this happened, the rest of the people on the island who had diseases also came and were cured (Acts 28:9).* |